COPING
CONTROVERSY

COPING WITH CONTROVERSY

HELPING CHRISTIANS HANDLE THEIR DIFFERENCES

Revised Edition

GARETH JONES

solway

First edition published 1994
by Vision Publications,
New Zealand

Second edition published 1996 by Solway

02 01 00 99 98 97 96   7 6 5 4 3 2 1

Solway is an imprint of Paternoster Publishing,
P.O. Box 300, Carlisle, Cumbria CA3 0QS, UK

British Library Cataloguing in Publication Data

A catalogue record for this book is available from the British Library

ISBN 1–900507–18–8

Typeset by Photoprint, Torquay, Devon
and printed in the U.K. by Cox & Wyman Ltd, Reading, Berkshire

Contents

PREFACE TO SECOND EDITION   ix

1. CONTROVERSY, CONFLICT AND STRIFE   1

   Stop beating me   1
   Definitions   4
   Condemned by rumour   5
   Heresy ousted   7
   Harmony disrupted   9
   I want to be positive   11
   Questions for group discussion   12

2. PERSONAL REFLECTIONS   14

   Why involve me in conflict?   14
   Ongoing conflict   16
   The centre of conflict   18
   Responding to conflict   22
   A false teacher?   25
   Where to, from here?   27
   Questions for group discussion   28

3. EVANGELICALS AND CONFLICT   29

   Divisions within evangelicalism   29
   At the boundaries of evangelicalism   31

Diversity within evangelicalism   32
Debate within evangelicalism   34
Confrontation   35
Pressure groups   37
Pragmatism and compromise   38
Public policy   40
Evangelicals and society   43
Questions for group discussion   45

4. JUDGING AND FORGIVING OTHERS   46

Destructive criticism   46
Seeing minor faults in others   47
Hypocrisy   49
False prophets and false teaching   53
Discernment   55
Taking account of the weak   57
Sacrificing precision on peripheral matters   61
Extent of God's forgiveness   62
Forgiveness within the Christian community   64
Extent of our forgiveness   68
Forgiveness and controversy   71
Questions for group discussion   72

5. LIVING FOR OTHERS   74

Unity in the body of Christ   74
The body of Christ and controversy   76
Humility   78
Putting the interests of others first   82
Living for one's opponents   83
Quarrels and dissension   85
Group factions   87
The dangers of speculation   91
Judgement and rebuke   94
The Holy Spirit and controversy   97
Salt and light   99
Questions for group discussion   102

6. LEARNING TO LIVE WITH CONTROVERSY   104

    Asking dangerous questions   104
    Making room for debate   107
    Pressure groups   110
    The dangers of dogmatism   114
    Freedom of expression   117
    Censorship   120
    Helping each other   124
    Questions for group discussion   127

7. WHERE SHOULD LINES BE DRAWN?   128

    Central or peripheral?   128
    Which option?   131
    More options   133
    Single-issue divisions   134
    Pastoral implications   136
    Am I making matters too complex?   139
    Knowing where to draw lines   141
    Questions for group discussion   145

8. THE ENJOYMENT OF DIFFERENCE   147

    Life in Lifdyl   147
    Parables and problem issues   149
    The pros and cons of being passionate 152
    Should there be boundaries?   156
    Which of us hasn't a few minor heresies? 158
    Making ourselves vulnerable   159
    In praise of dissent   161
    The challenge of Lifdyl   163
    Questions for group discussion   165

BOOKS FOR FURTHER READING   167

INDEX OF SCRIPTURE REFERENCES   170

Preface to second edition

I am a Christian employed as the Professor and Head of a moderate-size university department; my academic interests are in biological, medical and ethical issues. I am concerned with the study of the brain and the human body, biomedical ethics, and the interrelationship between my Christian faith and these other areas.

For many years I have attempted to have a Christian view on my activities. However, it has not been easy. Many of these areas are controversial, especially within Christian circles, and as a result I have had to face conflict and censorship there.

I could have avoided these areas, and neither spoken nor written about them. I could have dealt with them in purely secular ways, refusing to analyse them from a Christian viewpoint. Alternatively, I could have investigated them from a Christian angle, but stopped short of publishing my conclusions, leaving my thoughts in the form of questions and so hiding my own conclusions. Such an approach makes criticism of the writer or speaker much more difficult but it fails to take serious responsibility for the analysis. For me, that would not have been an honest approach. I think it is essential to

ix

work out a possible approach, whereby Christians can have the space for voicing informed conclusions, however difficult this may be when the areas are uncharted ones.

Later in this book I shall probe deeper into the matter and draw out principles to guide and direct Christians when confronted by issues where controversy is rife.

The controversies with which I shall be dealing stem from *differences in beliefs and attitudes* among Christians: disagreements over the role of women in society and in the church; the legitimacy or otherwise of using conventional or nuclear weapons as deterrents; economic policies and attitudes towards the poor; the status of the human embryo and foetus; the age of the earth and the role of evolutionary explanations in biology and geology; the necessity or otherwise of speaking in tongues or healing as manifestations of God's blessing; and many other aspects of prophecy, church government, and church affairs. The easiest path is that of separation and isolation. We simply refuse to have anything to do with those with whom we disagree, as individuals and as churches. We go our own way, ignoring these other Christians, avoiding fellowship with them, and all too often, giving the impression we would be happier if we never had to think about them.

My argument in this book is that such an approach is totally inadequate. It fragments the body of Christ and destroys the unity that should be ours. Therefore I shall refer to the divisive issues with which I am concerned as *secondary* or *peripheral* issues, the type of issues I have already mentioned. Such issues, while perfectly legitimate matters for debate and serious discussion, should never be allowed to divide those who agree on the central issues of the Christian faith, particularly concerning the person and work of Christ.

When I first decided to write this book I was unable to find any other books on this subject. It seemed to be a topic which evangelical Christians studiously avoided. While so many were embroiled in conflict of one sort or another, it seemed that very few people were prepared to face up to it. Over the last few years, however, this has been changing, and books with titles such as *Build That Bridge, When Christians Clash,* and *One in the Truth?* have appeared. I am delighted at this trend, and yet these books largely ignore the focus of my own thoughts. While dealing with conflict at a personal level, or between churches or church groupings, they have little to say about coping with the conflict stemming from real differences in beliefs. Richard Mouw's *Uncommon Decency* has touched on some of the issues of concern to me. He acknowledges the difficulty of holding to Christian convictions *and* treating vindictive opponents with civility and decency. My task is a similar one, although the contexts of our books are very different.

This is a personal book. It is quite unlike my other writings, such as *Our Fragile Brains, Brave New People, Manufacturing Humans* and *Brain Grafts.* Personally I have come face to face with conflict within the church. And it is that conflict which has driven me to write this book. I am not qualified to write a book on the historical aspects of conflict within Christendom or a theological treatise on conflict and unity. I very much hope that others appropriately qualified, will write such books with the present one intended as nothing more than a tentative beginning.

In the preface to the first edition, published in New Zealand, I expressed my thanks to those people who had encouraged me to persevere with the book. I was especially grateful to members of my family for supporting me in many ways; also for living with me through the episodes that led to the experiences recorded in the second chapter of the book. My thanks went to Barbara Telfer for going meticulously through all the chapters and for commenting in detail on the text.

That edition aroused considerable interest in New Zealand and, in more limited ways, in other countries. The present edition has been modified in various ways in response to comments, the major changes being additional first and last chapters, the omission of chapter 7 of the first edition, and the inclusion of further questions for group discussion at the end of each chapter. I am very grateful to the editorial team at Paternoster Press for their support and suggestions.

ONE

Controversy, Conflict and Strife

Stop beating me

> I don't mean to be a complainer, and I realize that I'm overly sensitive to this type of issue. It's probably because I've been beaten up too many times in my local church for trying to be an honest scientist and Christian.

So wrote an ordinary Christian on an internet group of Christians and scientists. He had had enough of being pilloried by fellow-Christians in the church he attended for his views on Christianity, creation and evolution. He felt there was a lack of openness on this issue. There was a correct position, and those who failed to adopt that correct position were chastised and shown the error of their ways. There was no opportunity for open discussion, no acknowledgement that there may be a variety of legitimate interpretations of crucial biblical passages. No wonder there is controversy in churches.

If this was a single isolated example of the problem, it wouldn't be worth devoting a book to it. But far from it. Look through the news sections of some Christian magazines, and more than likely you will encounter illustra-

1

tion after illustration of the problem. I did this, and it didn't take many issues to come up with a long list of examples of conflict. The headings alone gave the game away. In some of these cases, I've changed the names and a few of the details, so that the instances remain as anonymous as possible; but the strife remains as obvious as in the original:

> Hunting for heresy: prominent evangelicals come under
>   withering attack for controversial writings.
> Conflict divides leaders.
> Vote overturns women's ordination.
> Moderate wing of denomination takes flight.
> Dean's dismissal draws faculty, student protests.
> Seminary president booted.
> Ministry resolves wrongful termination suit.
> Movement grows amid doctrinal disputes.
> Homosexuality debate strains campus harmony.
> Evangelical theologians clash in public.
> Personnel woes persist at ministry centre.
> Faculty complaint clouds college accreditation.

All these headings refer to churches, Christian colleges or seminaries, or Christian organizations. None of the issues touches on central Christian beliefs. This is not to say they are unimportant, or that we should ignore them; not at all. They all need to be faced and resolved, or accommodated in some way. It would be foolhardy of me to suggest that they should be swept under the carpet.

What does concern me is the manner in which we face up to those differences that divide us within the church. The issues may be big doctrinal ones like the nature of Christ's resurrection body, or homosexuality. Others stem from an inability to exist alongside those with slightly different emphases, or they revolve around straightforward personal problems leading to repeated dissension within the church.

But why should this be? Some say it's inevitable. 'Don't worry, we are all sinful, what else can you expect?' Others remind us that this happened even among Jesus' own disciples. And it's gone on, unabated, through the centuries, as one Christian has fought another and as one group has torn another to shreds.

Some may be satisfied with this; I'm not. As we shall see later, my concern is with conflict over minor issues, not the big central ones at the heart of Christianity. I'm not going to debate how we cope with those who deny the claims Christ made for himself while insisting on still calling themselves Christians. I'm interested in the little things that divide us, in why we are so often prepared to go to war with each other over small matters. One writer put it like this:

> Strife among Christians persists, and, so often as not, such intramural disputes contain more vitriol than do disputes with non-Christians. Now, in an era of nearly instantaneous worldwide communication, attacks by self-appointed heresy hunters have escalated through the use of radio, television, newsletters, e-mail, fax machines, handbills, and other low-budget means to rally an audience against specific Christian leaders or ministries.

What is worrying is the frequency with which the condemnation is made public before any serious attempt has been made to discuss the matter with the accused. The dispute immediately hits the headlines, since this is part and parcel of the condemnation. Disputes handled in this way look far more like witch-hunts, than serious attempts to talk the matter through between equals.

All too often, what we see are narrow-minded, self-appointed arbiters of legalism sitting in judgement on Christians who say or do things of which they disapprove. They exist by using unfair and personal attacks on well-known Christians, and they may even spread vilification and untruths in order to get their message across. Their goal appears to be to silence the victim or elicit a recantation, even if it involves misrepresentation.

Definitions

I'll mainly be discussing *controversy*, with its emphasis on debate or dispute, especially in public or in the media. I didn't set out to limit myself to public disagreements, but the reality is that so many of the disagreements within Christian circles are public ones. They get out into the community; they are known about by those outside the church. All too often, a church has a reputation within its community for the difficulties it experiences in coping with its members or its pastor. On some occasions churches may wish to be known for the hard line they take with their members who fail to toe the party line. Too often, the claims and opinions of one side are pitted against those of another; 'correct' opinions are stacked against the 'incorrect' ones; it becomes 'us' against 'them'.

Conflict refers to sharp disagreements or clashes, especially between divergent ideas, interests or people. It also refers to the distress caused by mental struggles resulting from incompatible or opposing impulses. It makes us think of a hostile encounter of some kind; there is a fight and a prolonged struggle. It has the overtones of war and battles, with allies on one side and enemies on the other. Inevitably, each side is out for victory. Unfortunately, this is all too apt a description of some of the battles encountered within the church. What could be harmless disagreements readily become outright battles.

Strife has similar overtones — of bitter and sometimes violent conflicts or dissensions. Once again, only victory for one side and defeat for the other will suffice. There is antagonism, enmity and discord; there is competition — not the friendly rivalry of sport, but the contest of the battlefield.

Even if you think I have been melodramatic in these definitions, and even if you think I am exaggerating, the battle analogy cannot be entirely dismissed. I wish it could be. I wish I didn't have to discuss this topic. I wish all was sweetness and light. But it is not.

My use of this language is done deliberately and reluctantly. I cannot avoid it. Controversy, conflict and strife are endemic within Christian circles. Even if this is true of all other areas within society, as it undoubtedly is, that does not justify their presence within the church. I shall justify this statement in a later chapter. For now, we simply have to accept its grim reality.

Condemned by rumour

Let us imagine George Detas. He is a well-known speaker in Christian circles. Although he started out as a pastor, he is best known for his contemporary ministry to young people; he has a way with them; a knack of getting under their skins. He can speak their language and his ability to translate difficult theological ideas into concepts to which they can relate, has given him a well-deserved reputation. He is accepted on platforms where no theologian and few pastors could possibly go. But George's path is not an easy one. Frequently he speaks on 'risky' subjects in his attempt to work through exactly what Christian thinking has to offer in the nitty-gritty of everyday life. And this often lands him in trouble, because his words and phrases are sometimes misinterpreted.

George's approach takes him far away from accepted theological phrases and jargon. There's no point in using phrases that are well understood only by mature Christians, well-grounded in theological niceties, but which are meaningless to young people with no background in Christian things. George argues that he has to walk on thin ice because this is where his ministry takes him. Were he to fail to do this, his lines of communication would be cut off and his ministry would disappear.

George is unconventional. For this reason some Christians accuse him of error and have done their best to bring his ministry to an end. To them he is an apostate and they see it as their duty to condemn him publicly and forcefully. They consider that he is leading people astray; the quicker he is off the scene the better. Much of their criticism revolves around sexual matters; precisely what George does and does not see as allowed in terms of sexual conduct. There are also problems with his political views which are too left-wing for some Christians, and with his stance on scientific issues where they consider he has been taken in by secular thinking. In short, George is accused of being too much at ease in the world of unbelief.

Some organizations have responded to these criticisms and have withdrawn their speaking invitations. They feel it is too dangerous to be associated with such a theologically liberal and dangerous speaker. He may lead their young people astray. What is worst about his situation is that most of the condemnation to which George is subjected is based on rumour. He is denounced from afar, and repeatedly misrepresented. The picture of him which is promoted is one that his friends and close associates fail to recognize. He is accused of believing things he does not believe and of having attitudes that are far removed from all he stands for. The misrepresentations are many, and the smear tactics are tragic.

What is even more tragic is that the disinformation campaigns succeed. He is asked to leave a number of prominent committees and his ministry comes to a virtual halt. He does continue, but the thrust of his ministry has gone. The condemnation has succeeded and he is isolated as a suspicious, and rather disreputable, character. Most of the Christian organizations that used to sponsor him, stop doing so, in case they themselves become targeted as suspicious. He has been all but destroyed by malicious rumour, circulated in the name of Christ.

Heresy ousted

David Specks is a chemistry lecturer at Mappas Christian School, which prides itself on being evangelical and orthodox. He has been at this school for eight years and has given very faithful service over these years. He is known to be a good teacher; he is liked by the students and undertakes all his duties very competently. Being in a Christian school, he has opportunities in his teaching to discuss applied aspects of the Christian faith. These centre on ecological issues, which stem in part from his subject of chemistry. No problems are encountered with any of this teaching.

However, he also teaches senior students a course on 'Christian responsibility in the Modern World'. In this he covers subjects which range more widely, including creation and evolution; the new reproductive technologies and genetics; and gender issues, including homosexuality and women in leadership roles in society and the church. Many of these are contentious issues and, while it does not have any explicit printed policy on any of them, the school tends towards a conservative and traditional stance in practice.

David is always careful not to offend anyone if he can possibly help it. But he aims to make his teaching and seminars relevant for the students, so that they will be able to cope with the secular society which they will be entering very shortly. He believes that current issues should be well thought through and that Christians should know the arguments that non-Christians will use against them and their beliefs. He never aims to shock, but he does aim to be scrupulously honest. He likes working in a Christian

environment because this is an opportunity to demonstrate the relevance of biblical teaching to students,
both Christian and non-Christian.

David also believes in academic freedom. He considers that since he is a committed Christian, the other
teachers and the school authorities should trust his
judgement. However, when the parents of one of the
girls complain about the discussion in one of his
seminars, his judgement is questioned. He is given no
opportunity to explain what was said or the basis on
which he conducts his seminars. The Chairman of the
governors contends that the school is run on the basis
of the exclusivity of the Christian gospel, and in
opposition to three things — abortion, homosexuality,
and evolution. The fact that these three issues have
never been raised before or discussed in recent years,
is ignored in discussions with David. He is disciplined
and instructed to stop running seminars.

David is deeply upset because he does not hold
particularly radical views in any of these areas, although he remains unconvinced about the seven days
of creation and some of the interpretations based on
these. He only wants to be biblical in all his viewpoints, do his very best for the students and demonstrate to them that you can be a thinking person and a
committed Christian.

On the other hand, the governors now want to
ensure that just one viewpoint is held on these particular issues, and that the students are told the same
thing by all staff members. They believe they are
taking a strong moral stand, and that David has let
down the school. Other teachers come to David's
defence, as well as a number of parents. They all
reckon that he has been treated insensitively and in a
heavy-handed way. The governors, however, reaffirm
the traditional school basis (even though it has not
been formulated in recent years), and state that
teachers such as David are undermining the institution.

In view of these developments, David resigns. He is unwilling to have his Christian credentials disputed in this way. He is quickly employed by another school, this time a secular one, as deputy principal. Meanwhile the Mappas Christian School advertises for a replacement, and the job description is specific about the limitations within which the chemistry master will have to operate in seminars outside the field of chemistry.

Harmony disrupted

In 1970 Stodworth Evangelical Church came into existence and within three to four years became the most vigorous church in town. It was known to be open and welcoming. The ministry was firmly biblical, and was recognized as being strongly supportive of people in all walks of life and in many forms of Christian ministry. By 1975 it had two pastors who complemented each other very well. Under their ministry the church grew rapidly and was widely recognized, both within church circles and in the community at large, as a loving and caring community. It reached out into the community with its playgroup, meals for underprivileged, and primary school. Many outside the church contacted the pastors when in need of counselling.

The church was characterized by the wide variety of people it attracted. People came from different strata of society; it attracted young and old, students as well as retired people; blue-collar workers and professionals; single mothers, families with young children, and childless couples. There was an active group of singles, and regular opportunities to discuss all sorts of issues. Nothing, it seemed, was above ardent discussion.

The members of the church held an enormous breadth of views. For some, spiritual healing was very important; others set little store by this. Some in the church wanted to see far more women in leadership roles (besides the two women elders); others would have been happier to have had only men in the leadership team. Some wanted to see far more opportunities for the exercise of spiritual gifts; others thought the church was already going a little overboard in the charismatic area. Some were ardent pro-lifers, who would go on anti-abortion rallies in the town; others kept out of these debates because they could not subscribe to this emphasis. The church services were fairly informal with a mixture of old and new; for some this was fine, but for others it was too informal.

The growth of the church stemmed from various sources. People with backgrounds in a variety of denominations and church traditions were impressed with what they saw and became part of the church. New people to the town flocked there, as did students from the local college. New Christians found a place in the church; a number had become Christians there. The biblical preaching proved challenging and stimulating.

This church ethos continued for some years, but began to crumble when the pastors moved on within a year or so of each other. Unfortunately, each was replaced by a pastor with an authoritarian streak. This was unexpected and unplanned, and very soon the negative repercussions became evident. The openness disappeared overnight. The first episode of conflict arose when the pastors made it clear to the women elders that they should stand down. Only men were now looked upon for leadership in the church. The charismatic elements were downgraded, and soon disappeared altogether. It was suggested to an obstetrician in the congregation that he should cease speaking in public about abortion and the reproductive

Address:

Telephone:

① Situation that draws unity

Name:

Address:

② Civility and decency.

③ Lack of openness ː no opportunity for open discussion

④ Coffee beans.

Name:

Address:

Telephone:

⑤ Inevitably each side is out for victory

antagonism, enmity + discard

"being too much at ease with the w— of" unbelief

Name:

Address:

scrupulously honest

⑥ Maintain the ethos

Telephone:

⑦ The view of the psalts could not be challeng

① Attitude - unforgiving / hard hearts

② Speech - critical / forthful

③ Financial - absent

④ Acts for upbuilding - Any we seen as a
threat to the leadership?
was disarranged
On the surface all

⑤ Self righteousness - seemed well
but the atmosphere
had ch- dramatically

⑥ Secondary issues. ① dissatisfaction + unmet input

technologies, since his views were not those of the leadership and it was not his role to speak in opposition to the church's position on these matters. The church services became more formal since this was what the pastors wanted.

Many other issues arose and were dealt with in the same way. The views of the pastors could not be challenged. The discussion groups soon ceased to exist, as open discussion, led by church members, was discouraged. The pastors still preached biblically, even if the messages were less penetrating than under the old regime. Nevertheless, there was much that the congregation could learn. The tragedy was that anyone seen as a threat to the pastors was discouraged from leadership.

On the surface, all seemed well, but the atmosphere had changed dramatically. No longer were people affirmed for what they were; no longer was the diversity within the church celebrated; no longer were lay contributions to worship and leadership encouraged. Dissatisfaction became rampant. Stalwarts within the church began to drift away to other churches. Those on the periphery were no longer welcomed, unless they emerged as strong supporters of the pastors. The attendance at services dropped off and the community outreach diminished. A few new people came in, but, it was into a different church and their expectations were different.

Many people within the church were hurt, although the dissatisfaction remained under control. As people left, the pastors consolidated their position, since those remaining were more amenable to accept what they said. Central control was now established, and there was no longer even a hint of openness. The preaching still sounded biblical, but the heart of the church had been ripped out. All semblance of community had disappeared, and the church was but a pale reflection of its former self.

The sadness of this episode is not simply that a once flourishing institution has gone, but that Christ's body has been disrupted. The community around the church knows what has gone on, not in detail perhaps, but in enough detail to know that all is not well. After three years of disharmony and authoritarianism, the pastors' contracts were not renewed. The church more or less had to start again.

I want to be positive

All this is fine, you might say, but why read a book that is so negative? I want to be positive. Even if some of this is true, there are far brighter and happier things in the Christian life for me to read about. Leave me alone, and let me get on with the good things in the church. The church may not be perfect, but I don't want to read about its imperfections.

I sympathize with this, but only in the same way as I do with books on coping with cancer or depression or bereavement. We would all like to live without any of these, and perhaps some of us refuse to read about them. Yet, they are written in order to help people who cannot escape from it. Only the irresponsible ignore them; the responsible face up to them so that they can be as helpful and mature as possible. The Christian way is not one that ignores reality.

I would much prefer not to write about problem areas. The truth is I cannot avoid them. But my aim is to be as positive as possible, and I believe we can be positive. The problems, like the ones we have just encountered, are tragic, but there is a better way. The negative becomes a way into a positive, mature Christian approach to all those things that separate and hurt us in the church. But before we begin to travel along this path, I shall dwell just a little longer on the problems as I myself have encountered them.

Questions for group discussion

1. Think of as many examples as you can of issues that divide Christian churches and organizations. Why do you think these issues prove so divisive?

2. Do you agree that conflict within Christian circles is sometimes more bitter than in other circles. If so, what do you think the reasons might be?

3. Discuss candidly the three illustrations used in this chapter, those of George Detas, David Specks, and Stodworth Evangelical Church. Different members of the group should put themselves in the positions of: i) George Detas and one of his opponents, ii) David Specks and a member of the governing body, iii) a stalwart member of Stodworth Evangelical Church and one of the new pastors.

    What can you learn from these examples?

TWO

Personal Reflections

Why involve me in conflict?

Up until my late thirties I had lived under the fond illusion that I was the sort of person who did not become embroiled in controversial matters. I do not, by nature, go looking for arguments and I do not, generally, provide opinions on any and every subject under the sun. I am not known as the type of person who speaks first and thinks later.

The first significant occasion when I became the centre of controversy came as a rude shock. Like the other controversies in this book, it involved the Christian community. Quite unexpectedly, and completely against all my instincts and beliefs, I found myself cast as the centre of opposition to the pastor and leaders of the church to which my wife and I belonged. I was the leader of two groups within the church; a study/family group and a Bible study discussion group. Both these groups grew, and in both we rejoiced as we studied the Bible, discussed numerous questions concerned with church growth and the gifts of the Spirit, and shared together as individuals and families. We were open and honest with one another, and we assumed others would be the same.

But the church leadership considered us a threat. We had never questioned the authority of any of the leaders. Unfortunately, our willingness to look at all sorts of issues and attempt to assess them biblically, constituted unknown territory for the church leaders. We were seen to be questioning unspoken assumptions within the church, and this was disloyal. This was not our intention, and we were not departing from any basic doctrines.

Much to my dismay a rift had developed, and I had no idea how to deal with it. There was hurt on both sides, and in the end we did the unthinkable. My family left the church. The gulf that had arisen had nothing to do with any major doctrines. We went our separate ways because we could no longer coexist. Personality differences had some part to play; expectations regarding freedom of thought and the role of the ministry had a part to play. But these did not amount to anything that could not have been sorted out by forgiveness, reconciliation, and a growth in understanding on both sides.

Unfortunately, these did not take place. After almost twenty years the wounds of that episode have not completely left me. I can still remember the sense of complete rejection as I was told, by one of the church leaders, to leave — there was no place for me in that church anymore. I and my family had to find somewhere else.

We nearly didn't find somewhere else. That incident left us with grave doubts about the meaning of Christianity and its outworking in the church. The following nine months were hard ones as we sought to re-establish the meaning of the Christian faith in our lives, and in a corporate setting. Other families found themselves similarly affected, and finally we all found different church settings for the way forward.

All of us involved fell short. We all failed at reconciliation, and the church of Jesus Christ suffered as a result.

On the other hand, by the grace of God, many of us learned as well. For me, the loss of that time was the start of a reality in my Christian life I had never previously experienced. It also brought us into contact with Christians whose genuineness and graciousness opened up new dimensions of Christian acceptance which we, as a family, had seen little of prior to that time.

Ongoing conflict

Although I did not realize it at the time, that experience was to prove very helpful when controversy of an even more vicious nature struck me personally in 1984. There had been other isolated instances of controversy in the intervening years. One, in particular, stands out clearly in my mind. I was involved in a morning talk-back radio programme on creation and evolution. There were two guests in the studio — myself and a representative of a creation-science organization. We were both Christians and I imagine our theological positions on many, perhaps most, major doctrinal issues would have been the same. However, as far as this programme was concerned, we represented slightly different positions on the manner in which God brought the world into being. We were both creationists (in a theological sense), and yet we appeared to have no common ground.

We discussed and disagreed on the programme, just as we had discussed and disagreed on previous occasions. There is nothing wrong with this within Christian circles, just as there is nothing wrong with it within society at large. It is very important to be able to air one's differences; this is preferable to forcibly restraining expressions of concern and shying away from airing alternative viewpoints. The sadness I felt at the time was not that we held alternative interpretations of some passages in the Bible, but that both before and after the programme we had nothing to say to each other. Our relationship was characterized, not by the things that united us, but by those that divided us. We represented opposing 'camps' on this one issue, and it was this opposition that dominated our interaction. Although we must have been 'one in the faith', it seemed impossible to have fellowship, since the many points on which we would have agreed were thrust into the background by the one point on which we disagreed.

That morning I left the studios of the radio station deeply perplexed. What did Christian fellowship mean, when disagreement over one issue (however important some Christians may consider it to be) appeared to negate agreement over so many other issues? On both sides, the conflicting viewpoints were genuinely held. Neither of us was trying to be awkward, and it is difficult to believe that either of us was entirely without error. But, if we both claimed to be Christians whose faith was based on the Bible, did we really have nothing in common? Was there nothing we could say to each other, and more important, were there no ways in which we could actually help one another? Or was it inevitable that we go our separate ways, sniping at each other from time to time, and ignoring each other's existence at all other times?

Some months later, when engaged to speak on the interrelationship between creation and evolution in another city, letters starting appearing in a weekly Christian magazine warning people against attending because of the views I held. Such opposition may, of course, simply be a fact of life, and some might say: 'Be thick-skinned and get on with living; even Christians have their hang-ups'. Perhaps. That is what I did. Unfortunately I have never been able to view such a situation in these terms. For me, such situations should serve as a warning that there are forces within Christianity prepared to isolate one Christian from another on the basis of intellectual, cultural and attitudinal differences, and these forces disturb me.

On a personal level, I was beginning to realize I had been naive in thinking that I could go through life

without having enemies. Perhaps I had failed to take
sufficiently seriously the teachings of Jesus, when he
warned would-be disciples that following him would
usher in strife and turn people, even close relations,
against them. What took me by surprise, however, was
that the strife was between other Christians and me, not
between an antagonistic society and me. I was being
condemned by Christians, and it was other Christians
who were being warned about the dangers of listening
to what I had to say.

Unfortunately, controversies have characterized the
history of the church, and some of them have been very
bitter. Even worse, Christians of one persuasion have
been put to death by Christians of another persuasion.
In a former age I might have been burnt at the stake for
my views on creation and evolution! Whatever his-
torians make of such events, we cannot use those approaches as a basis for our actions and attitudes today.
Our guide is Scripture and the model presented by
Christ, not the actions of other humans.

The incidents I have just recounted are far from
world-shattering. But they were major enough for me,
especially since I had for so long harboured the grand
illusion that I was able to get on reasonably amicably
with most people. The inevitable person-to-person rivalries and disagreements, in most instances, were resolved
with time. Looking back, I realize they were not resolved in a specially Christian way, but they generally
were resolved.

The centre of conflict

All these previous experiences did not prepare me ade-
quately for June 1984, when the uproar over my book
Brave New People: Ethical issues at the commencement of life
erupted in the United States. I did not expect it, since, on
both sides of the Atlantic, considerable efforts had been
made during the editing of the manuscript to cope with

possible criticism of sensitive issues. The manuscript had been assessed by six readers, and I had modified what were seen as possible offending passages — sometimes to the extent of inserting explanations or illustrations I was not entirely happy with myself. In Britain the early reactions to the book's appearance were unexceptional. After all, the book was not intended to alienate would-be readers. The only purpose for writing it was to provide guidance for those struggling to come to terms with the burgeoning new reproductive technologies, especially as at that time very little such literature was available within evangelical circles.

However, to my utter astonishment, at 5am on Wednesday, 6 June 1984, I was woken by the ringing of the telephone at my bedside. An editor of the publisher in the United States was informing me that the book had been very severely criticized by an anonymous writer in the news-sheet of an evangelical anti-abortion pressure group. Later in the morning, when I was properly awake, an hour-long phone call spelled out the situation much more clearly. The criticism of *Brave New People* had been accompanied by a call for the group's supporters to write in to the publisher objecting to its publication.

And so the turmoil of the next few weeks commenced. Letters did indeed pour in to the publisher in the United States; there was even an anti-abortion demonstration outside its headquarters. A prominent evangelical leader advocated the boycotting of all the publisher's publications by booksellers in the United States, and some booksellers did precisely this. Finally, after a couple of months, *Brave New People* was withdrawn from the American market.

That, it may have seemed, was the end of this unsavoury incident. But it wasn't. *Brave New People* made a brief foray back into the American market before disappearing forever. I continued to receive critical comments, both publicly and privately, although my right to reply was severely circumscribed. The debate over such issues as the status of the foetus led me to write a sequel,

*Manufacturing Humans: The challenge of the new repro-
ductive technologies*, which was published in Britain but
never appeared in the American market. I became increasingly involved in ethical debates — in Christian
circles, in medical forums, and in society at large. And
perhaps most important of all, I was forced to consider
very seriously the issue central to this present book —
the means by which Christians cope with differences of
opinion and with the controversy that so often accompanies these.

What was it about *Brave New People* that elicited such
a vehement response in the United States? In 1984 there
had been little in the way of Christian writing on the
new reproductive technologies. And so, while the focus
of attention in the book was *in vitro* fertilization, my
discussions of artificial insemination, cloning, amnio-
centesis, genetic engineering, and the technological environment responsible for these developments, evoked
only limited reaction. I doubt whether many people who
were so critical of me had even read these chapters. The
furore was not over my treatment of these issues, but
over the one chapter that dealt with therapeutic (in-
duced) abortion. It was in this chapter that I had apparently transgressed all the principles of evangelicalism by
allowing for abortion under certain circumstances. A
few of my critics even stated that I wrote the book in
order to advance a liberal view of abortion.

I found that my 'heretical' views had earned me
notoriety within evangelical circles. Not only this, but, in
the eyes of some, my views were so dangerous they had
to be censored. And they were, since *Brave New People*
was withdrawn from the American market. The censorship was carried out by a few self-appointed guardians
of evangelical morality, who conducted a vociferous and
concerted campaign against the book, myself, and the
publisher.

I was accused of dishonesty and hypocrisy; it was said
that my chief aim was to advocate abortion. I was
accused of espousing humanism; my ethics were

claimed to be based on sentimentality, and aimed to pervert justice. My Christianity was questioned; one writer had few doubts that I was bound for hell. My position as an evangelical was denied, since I was said to endorse technological procedures and 'quality of life' concepts. My views were repeatedly compared to those of Hitler's eugenicists, and also to those of bygone slave-owners in the United States.

My critics had no doubt whatsoever that I advocated the murder of unborn children. I was labelled a eugenicist, who advocated death as a solution to social problems. Others had no hesitation in claiming that I advocated euthanasia and infanticide. Yet others claimed that I supported most (if not all) abortions requested by women. Such writers had no difficulty in making my views almost as liberal as they wished.

My motives were directly questioned; I was accused of writing in this vein in order to make money, or to infiltrate the evangelical wing of the church with theologically liberal views. What was significant is that those making such claims had never met me, and knew virtually nothing about me. It is also significant that only one of my critics wrote to me. Others were requested to do so, but I never heard from them. An attempt by one organization to set up a debate between one of my most forthright critics and myself, failed to eventuate when my critic declined the invitation. There is evidence that most of those who wrote to the publisher demanding that the book be withdrawn from publication had never read it, and probably had never seen it. Even some of the reviewers appeared to have read very little beyond the one chapter dealing with abortion.

There is no point in prolonging this litany of condemnation and harsh criticism. The crucial point is this: the condemnation and criticism were made in the name of Christ, and were intended to bring honour to him and his church. The critics considered themselves unequivocally to be right and the condemned unequivocally to be wrong. This was based on the assumption that they were God's true representatives whereas the condemned were unworthy of him, and were probably not Christians at all. What is significant is the certainty implicit within this condemnation. Those passing judgement were certain about the validity of their own set of beliefs, the purity of their own attitudes, and their authority to act as sole judge of the standing and integrity of other Christians. It is these certainties that I question in the remaining chapters of this book, since they lie at the heart of so much conflict within Christian circles.

Responding to conflict

How did I respond at the time, and how did others involved in the controversy react? Did we follow biblical principles? Was there any attempt at reconciliation?

As I contemplated the mounting criticism, my initial reaction was to be stunned. I found it impossible to consider the matter rationally for many months, and it was only after six months that I felt able to look again at the reams of critical reviews that had mounted up in my filing cabinet. By this time I had calmed down emotionally, and was able to stand back and assess what had happened.

As I did this, I could see something of the strength of the viewpoints that had been expressed, and when looked at *en masse* they appeared to question almost everything I stood for. I had no wish to escape the force of these criticisms, since they may have been true. But if they were true, I had to examine myself very seriously to see where I stood before the One I had long considered to be my Lord and my God. *Brave New People* was written as a Christian contribution to thinking through the implications of some of the new developments in biomedicine. But, was I appallingly wrong? Was I a Christian at all? Perhaps, as some of my critics asserted, I was a wolf in sheep's clothing; perhaps I was a humanist, and perhaps I did derive all my views and attitudes from human aspirations rather than from God. When severely indicted by other Christians, it is imperative to ask whether one has been deceived, and whether one's efforts to speak Christianly on issues within society are inherently flawed. These were possibilities that could not be overlooked. My critics may have been correct, and it may have been time for me to pack my bags as a Christian and accept that I had been misled all along.

An alternative conclusion could have been that I was a Christian, but not an evangelical. I had to take seriously the possibility that my approach to the Bible was substandard, as some of my critics had so forcefully told me. Perhaps I had failed abysmally in my exegesis of crucial biblical passages, had been unduly swayed by social pressures and by the pragmatism of my scientific training. Perhaps only professionally trained theologians can understand the Bible sufficiently well to make pronouncements on the beginnings of human life and on the moral status of the human embryo and foetus; I was not trained in theology.

A further possibility was that those critics who had castigated my contribution to the bioethical debate may themselves have been wrong. They may have been wrong in the condemnatory tone of their criticism, in the personal abuse hurled at me, and in the selective reading (or no reading at all) of *Brave New People*. They may also have been mistaken in thinking that their views were the only acceptable ones within evangelicalism. In short, their actions and attitudes were strange, if Christian.

As the person at the centre of this particular controversy, I found it impossible to escape from the logic of this confrontation. Either my own position and my attitudes were (and still are) anathema to true Christianity, or the attitudes of my most belligerent critics were impossible to reconcile with the standards of Christ. The dilemma here has nothing to do with the rightness or wrongness of either position on abortion, but with the ways in which we treat each other within the body of Christ. This is why the issue of conflict is much bigger than any specific example.

Of course, I may be too emotionally involved in this particular controversy, and so my analysis is an extreme one. Many Christians have been hurt by the criticisms of other Christians, and there have been many bitter controversies within the church. These people did not complain; why do I? Perhaps I am far too sensitive, and am unable to face up to the rigours and turmoil of debate. And my position is made worse if I will insist on standing apart from mainline evangelical thinking on ethical matters.

But I remain unconvinced. My critics allowed me no voice, whatsoever. Their main concern was to silence me, because they considered that what I had to say was a hindrance to them. They refused to debate issues — after all, they were right and I was wrong. They wanted me out of the way. *But wait a moment* — this whole episode took place within the body of Christ. The shape of the opposition and the nature of the campaign mounted against me, was a secular device, used for silencing embarrassing opponents; plenty of such games are played within the world of professional politics, international espionage, and high-stake business negotiations. But on this occasion the game was being played out within the Christian community, where the rules should be different. Or should they? I assumed they should be, and such an assumption drives this book.

What allowed this to come about? I was considered an intruder, someone without a contribution to make to the debate within evangelicalism. What I had to say was branded as unrepresentative of evangelical thinking. Consequently, it should not be allowed *as a contribution from within evangelicalism*. No evangelical publisher should publish such views; no evangelical church or para-church organization should provide room for the expression of such views. In other words, there is no place within evangelicalism and evangelical literature for the contribution of someone like me.

This is a process of exclusion, carried out by a few people who consider themselves the true representatives of an evangelical position. It requires no reference to the person concerned. They are so confident of the correctness of their standpoint that no debate is either necessary or allowable. All alternative arguments to the 'correct' ones are so dangerous that ordinary Christians must be shielded from them. There is no room for other opinions or for dialogue.

This process of exclusion can be carried out in the context of any issue. Bioethical issues concerned me in this particular instance. But why not over economic issues, or creation-evolution ones, or the inerrancy of Scripture, or the gifts of the Spirit, or aspects of prophecy, or the role of women in the ordained ministry, or nuclear deterrence? At one time or another, all these are the subject of similar processes of exclusion by self-appointed 'guardians of the faith'. My experience, therefore, is just one of many, all of which raise precisely the same issues, and all of which result in confrontation within the community of God's people.

In each case, the arguments of the critics, regardless of who they may be, are exclusive ones. It is they who are the representatives of true Christianity, whereas those they are criticizing are threats to true Christianity and are false teachers. In the *Brave New People* incident, it was I who was regarded as a threat to true Christianity and it was I who was cast in the role of a false teacher.

A false teacher?

But was I? Am I? These questions forced me to consider very seriously whether my critics were indeed correct. I had to work on the assumption that I was a false teacher, and that I was a wolf in sheep's clothing. And so, over the months following the outburst over the book, I examined numerous biblical passages dealing with false teachers and false teaching, and the conclusion I came to was an 'either/or' one: either I was a false teacher, or some at least of my critics were. I was deeply disturbed by such a conclusion, since I regarded my critics as brothers and sisters in Christ. It was I who was faced with the possibility of being a false teacher, not them. But I found I could make no headway, until I accepted the conclusion to which I had very reluctantly come: that both those being judged and those making the judgement had to look very carefully at their respective standings before Christ. After much prayer and agonizing, I concluded, rightly or wrongly, that my position did not make me a false teacher.

It had become obvious to me, though, that both my critics and I were (and are) responsible before Christ for our beliefs, our teaching, and our attitudes. After considerable thought and prayer I was able to regard them as much as Christ's representatives as I thought I was. I also came to the conclusion that, if they denied my standing in Christ, that was a matter between themselves and their Lord. Nevertheless, I couldn't escape from the conclusion that if they were prepared to divide the body of Christ over these matters, the question of false teaching could not be completely overlooked. And this is why a book such as the current one is relevant.

My feelings about this particular controversy are of concern to me and are not particularly relevant to most other people. But there are far broader issues at stake, and it is these that cannot be ignored by the church at large. No, they can be ignored, but if they are we ignore something of crucial significance for the health of the church, and for the witness of God's people.

Let's return to *Brave New People* to complete the story. More than a year after that fateful day in June 1984, my only personal account of the incident appeared in the *Journal of the American Scientific Affiliation*. This article was reprinted in a British publication, and so appeared on both sides of the Atlantic. I know there was much initial foreboding in the United States about publishing it, for fear of the negative reactions it might elicit. In the event, however, the response to it was both positive and considerable. It seemed to touch a nerve with many people; it was dealing with a theme many people had encountered. Disappointingly, none of my critics responded to it or dealt, in any context, with the issues I raised. For me, the sadness of the situation lies in the little regard such writers had for my integrity as a human being, let alone as a Christian.

Once more, we are back at fundamental questions revolving around the nature of our oneness in Christ. This is of the utmost importance in determining how we deal with differences of opinion, conflict of interests, within the Christian community.

Where to, from here?

It is now time to dig deeper, and pick up the loose threads of the instances we've looked at in these first two chapters. I am a Christian working in a secular environment, where I interact with people of many persuasions, as well as with Christians both there and in churches. My interests are such that I deal repeatedly with issues that divide both society and the church.

What I say will have relevance to divisions that split churches, and yet this is not the focus of my concern. I shall not deal with the divisions between denominations, however important these may be. First and foremost my concern is with the workplace, and with the way in which Christians function in the workplace and society, and with the way in which they deal, as Christians, with divisive issues. However, once this happens, it has repercussions for them as Christians within the Christian community. Ideally, we should be speaking from our base within the church to the society within

which we live and work, but when our speaking and
acting touch on contentious matters, tensions rapidly
emerge.

Since I'm writing as an evangelical Christian, I first
have to look at what is understood by this term. How is
it defined in the context of different opinions on secondary matters? Has it allowed for divergences of viewpoints?

Questions for group discussion

1. Have you ever left one church for another? If you
    have, what have been the reasons? If it has involved
    hurt and misunderstanding, how have you and
    others dealt with these? If you have never left a
    church, how have you responded when others have
    done so?

2. Are there any issues that you think are sufficiently
    important to justify breaking fellowship with an-
    other Christian? If there are, what are they?

3. As a group, discuss one instance of serious con-
    troversy in which one of you has been involved, or
    which you have experienced at first hand. What
    were some of the major features that contributed to
    it? Could it have been avoided in the first place?
    How was it handled? What were some of its reper-
    cussions?

4. How do you respond when a Christian bookshop
    has a policy not to stock certain books, even though
    they are written by evangelical Christians? Exam-
    ples might be books that are strongly anti-
    Charismatic, or that recognize a place for an
    evolutionary mechanism (come up with your own
    favourites).

THREE

Evangelicals and Conflict

Divisions within evangelicalism

My starting point is evangelicalism, since this is where I come from. This is a movement or tradition within the church, committed to the historic Protestant understanding of Christianity. It has divided from groups with various liberal theological positions, on the ground that these have compromised essential elements of the gospel. As a result, various beliefs have emerged as its hallmarks, including the personal nature of God and the existence of three persons in the Godhead; God as creator of all that exists and his sovereignty in revelation, redemption and final judgement. Other beliefs include the central place of the Bible as God's revelation of himself and his purposes, and its authority in matters of faith and conduct. Basic to evangelicalism's view of human nature is the sinfulness and guilt of human beings, with redemption being made possible by Christ's death on the cross and his resurrection from the dead; believers look forward to the personal return of Christ. The indwelling of the Holy Spirit in the believer is seen as crucial to the Christian life.

Until the 1960s evangelicals were relatively few in number, and constituted a minority force concerned with their own survival. As long as this situation remained, they were relatively homogeneous in attitudes and outlook. There were theological and denominational differences, and on occasion these proved tragically divisive, but these differences were regarded as secondary to the central issues on which most evangelicals were united. As an embattled minority, the distinction between evangelicals on the one side and liberals on the other was clearly seen and was codified in well-defined doctrinal statements that enshrined distinct points of demarcation between the two camps.

Nevertheless, doctrinal statements were almost as important for what they omitted as for what they included. For instance, they omitted a large range of issues, such as baptism, church government, prophecy, the charismata, predestination, and creationism. It was not that these matters were considered unimportant, but that they were regarded as of secondary importance alongside the major evangelical doctrines concerning the character of God, the person and work of Jesus Christ, the reality of sin and the fall, the work of the Holy Spirit, and the nature of the Christian hope. Many within evangelicalism were only too aware that the secondary issues were capable of creating wedges within the evangelical consensus. Were this to happen, the ability of evangelicalism to cross denominational barriers would soon be eroded.

Over the last 35 years there has been a burgeoning in the influence of conservative Christianity. From being a minority influence in Protestantism, evangelicalism has become a major ecclesiastical force in many countries. However, this growth in strength has proved a mixed blessing, since it has been accompanied by diversification of the evangelical consensus. This has taken two forms. One has been a broadening of the limits of evangelicalism; the other has been a splitting up of evangelicalism by the formation of subgroups within it. Although these two movements appear to have been at loggerheads, the one blurring the distinctions between evangelicals and those outside evangelicalism, and the other emphasizing an increasing number of distinctives within evangelicalism, both are relevant to my discussion. This is because both have led to controversy within evangelicalism.

At the boundaries of evangelicalism

While many evangelicals were once characterized by a cultural ghetto mentality, this is no longer a universal phenomenon. As evangelicalism has increasingly become accepted and respectable, there has been a tendency in some circles for the demarcation between evangelicals and non-evangelicals to become blurred. Healthy as this may be, evangelicals are no longer as readily recognizable as they once were. This has had implications for what they regard as acceptable social and moral standards, and even for the theological boundaries of evangelicalism itself.

It has spawned other trends. For instance, evangelicalism has had the opportunity to flourish and delve into areas, questions and issues previously closed to it. This has been highly relevant to my own experiences, since I am a product of contemporary evangelicalism and have felt able to tackle many of the questions confronting modern society in the areas of biology and medicine. I have also felt able to approach these questions *as an evangelical Christian*, and I have been willing to outline new solutions when confronted by new questions.

Such an approach does, of course, have its dangers, and these are evident to me, to people like me, and far more so to others within evangelicalism who are sceptical about this approach. Herein lies a potent cause of division. It's possible for someone like myself to ignore,

however inadvertently, the boundaries of evangelicalism, and adopt what some may regard as a liberal stance
on biomedical and moral questions. But where do the
boundaries lie? It's far from satisfactory criticizing
someone for overstepping the boundaries, if there has
been no serious discussion of where these are found.
Even such discussions may prove divisive.

The boundaries of evangelicalism have never been
clearly drawn in the areas of many contentious contemporary issues. What I and others like me are doing, is to
propose where they might be placed. But this is no easy
matter, and in many instances there is little agreement.
Consequently, what should be a matter for discussion
can all too easily become yet another source of division.
Even worse, to some evangelicals anyone prepared to
enter into serious discussion of modern trends within
society, technology, and ethics, rather than automatically
opposing such trends, has already forsaken the faith.

These tensions surface when it becomes apparent that
some evangelicals are prepared to *explore* new territory,
whereas others wish to view the new territory in terms
of old, well-established ideas. This is sometimes viewed
as a conflict between non-biblical answers (the new
explorations) and biblical ones (the traditional answers).
Whenever the distinction is viewed like this, conflict is
inevitable. To state that a position is not biblically-based
is tantamount to denying that it is an evangelical position, even when the issue in question is a peripheral
one.

Diversity within evangelicalism

The other side of the coin is the emergence of special
interest groups. The relative homogeneity of evangelicalism has disappeared, and has been replaced by an
increasing diversity of groups with their own narrow
distinctives. Distinctives only become a problem when

they serve as barriers to isolate the groups from one another and from evangelicalism as a whole. When this occurs, the consequences are serious, since distinctives are frequently put forward as having biblical authority. And so, by definition, those groups or individuals lacking the distinctive in question are regarded by others as failing to live up to the standards of Scripture. The potential for fragmentation is considerable, and it all too readily takes place in a spirit of criticism and animosity.

Fragmentation is closely allied with concern for the purity of the church. This is good, since without it there would be no evangelicalism today. The strength of the tradition has been to ensure the survival of biblical emphases. The weakness of the tradition has been to allow the emergence of churches and church groupings with increasingly narrow foci of interest and concern. And it is these weaknesses that have come increasingly to the fore as evangelicalism has increased in strength and has had to concern itself less and less with attacks from outside.

The appearance of an increasing number of divisions within evangelical ranks is illustrated by recent debates. These have made much of issues such as biblical inerrancy and its role as a hallmark of evangelical orthodoxy, the place of social justice within the church, the role of women within the ministry, and the extent to which evangelical local churches should co-operate with theologically liberal churches and denominations. Additional issues ask whether the charismatic movement has a contribution to make to evangelicalism, the legitimacy or otherwise of nuclear deterrence, the nature of biblical revelation with regard to science — particularly with regard to the mechanism of creation and the age of the world. And there is an ever-increasing list of biomedical issues, bringing into focus the meaning of human existence and the degree of control to be exercised over human life.

Debate within evangelicalism

Debate over these and many other questions is healthy, and should be encouraged. Evangelicalism should be characterized by vigorous debate, since it has a contribution to make to the thinking and attitudes of the wider Christian community and also because evangelicals should be aware of the nuances of debate in these areas. This is only true, however, if genuine debate is occurring. It is all too easy for monologue to occur under the guise of debate, with the *correct answer* being provided for the faithful, and all other contributions being deemed unworthy of serious consideration. When this is the state of affairs, the issues themselves become divisive, marking off the 'faithful' from the 'unfaithful'. Unfortunately, it does not take much reading of evangelical books and magazines to realize that the issues I have just referred to are, all too frequently, approached in an authoritative 'correct/incorrect' manner. This leads to division and loss within evangelicalism, rather than to enriched understanding by the movement as a whole.

Differences of approach to these issues lead to division only when the issues themselves are exalted to primary status. Not one of these issues has traditionally featured as a doctrine distinctive of evangelical Christianity. However, once they are used to divide evangelicals from one another, they have been elevated to the same status as that of central beliefs. Christians who regard themselves as evangelicals can be excluded from fellowship with other evangelicals because of differences in their views on any of these matters. This is true, even if they hold identical views on the person and work of Christ, and even if their lives testify to the indwelling work of the Holy Spirit.

Modern evangelicalism is rife with such divisions, with all the detrimental consequences that inevitably follow for the life both of the church and of individual Christians. It's my contention that the existence of this multiplicity of divisions should be a matter of considerable concern. And yet I sense that all too many Christians accept the existence of these divisions with what appears to be consummate ease. For me this is a matter of even greater concern than the divisions themselves. There is little, if anything, most of us can do about the historic denominational divisions within the church. But such divisions are far outstripped by the new divisions we are constantly creating in our contemporary world. They occur because we are willing to separate from Christians of like mind, of similar aspirations regarding central Christian affirmations, because we disagree on a far less crucial matter.

Confrontation

Political, union, and academic forums are dominated by confrontation, with one rigid stance pitted against another. Inherent in much of this confrontation is pungent criticism, which sometimes goes as far as to cast grave doubt on the integrity and even sanity of the opponents. Taken to this extreme, criticism becomes a means of hiding one's own mediocrity by preventing thoughtful, reasoned argument. Whenever taken this far, institutions and people are placed at risk, since all forms of constructive, serious debate have been outlawed.

Far away from such extremes, confrontation is often part and parcel of everyday existence. But when issues are seen as black and white, right and wrong, confrontation becomes inevitable since the possible perspectives are narrowed down to just two — conservative and liberal, traditionalist and radical, the dries and the wets — no matter what the topic is. There can be no mediating position. What is crucial is that a conservative stance tends to view any moderately conservative position as liberal, whereas a liberal stance views all moderately liberal positions as conservative.

An example from my own area of interest illustrates this point. With regard to the status of the human embryo and the extent to which it should be protected, a conservative position tends to be strongly pro-embryo (and hence anti-research), whereas a liberal position is strongly pro-research (with little regard being paid to the protection of the embryo). That is fine for advocates of the extreme positions. The problem comes with the way in which advocates of the extremes view more moderate positions.

One would expect a moderately conservative position to fit fairly close to the conservative end of the scale. In practice, however, confrontational attitudes from a conservative perspective interpret a moderately conservative position as though it was pro-research and indistinguishable from a liberal position that advocates unfettered embryo research. This is both misleading and untrue; any differences between the moderately conservative and the conservative are small compared with those between the moderately conservative and liberal.

The process applies to other areas as well: including theology. The apparent dichotomy between the sovereignty of God and freedom of the human will can readily become a major gulf between two systems of thought. When taken to extremes they become mutually exclusive, with room only for one view: it is either the sovereignty of God and no human freedom, or complete freedom of the will and no room for God's sovereignty. The end result is that biblical teaching has been converted into some all-encompassing system of thought, which comes to assume greater importance than biblical revelation.

The immense danger of this type of approach is that it is based on the assumption that ethical decisions, theological positions, or social viewpoints, are arrived at entirely by logic. That is why only two positions are allowed for: a pro- and an anti-position; in favour of some proposition or against it. Not only this, but it allows opponents of a position to predict corollaries of that position — regardless of whether the holders of the position agree or not. This is precisely what happened with *Brave New People*; many of my detractors argued that my position leads to abortion on demand, infanticide, and euthanasia. They were thinking in these logical terms, and were convinced that this type of progression always occurs.

This may have a compulsion of sorts, but it overlooks the complex nature of ethical decision-making or, for that matter, the complex nature of biblical revelation and of theology. For instance, to believe that warfare to defend the legitimate interests of one's own society is justified, does not automatically justify all modern wars, every form of nuclear deterrence, and biological warfare. Logic may suggest that all these other stances follow inevitably from the general perspective allowing warfare under certain circumstances, but social policy, theology, and common sense do not suggest so.

Pressure groups

Pressure groups are formed in order to advocate a single cause. They may represent a wide array of interested parties brought together to contend for this cause, or they may represent a much narrower constituency (such as evangelicals) having as their goal the overturning of a particular practice within society. The question for us is how pressure groups fit into the general evangelical scene and whether, by their very nature, they tend to be divisive forces within evangelicalism.

Evangelical pressure groups have to reckon with the major danger of being identified too closely with Christianity itself. Whenever this occurs, the seeds of division and controversy have been well and truly sown. Since pressure groups have as their object the forwarding of a social cause, the danger is that the cause may be elevated to a position on a par with Christ. By its very nature, the cause may unite some Christians while alienating others. Whenever this happens, an end result of pressure group activity is that it succeeds in identifying supporters as 'friends', while converting non-supporters into 'enemies'. And this happens even when those non-supporters are fellow-Christians, who may agree, largely, with the cause in question.

The issue for Christians is whether pressure groups, by their very nature, are in line with biblical attitudes and perspectives. Or do they owe more to secular attitudes of confrontation than to biblical attitudes of mutual understanding and reconciliation?

Pressure groups have a tendency to dogmatism, since complex issues are reduced to a single component lending itself to 'yes/no' responses. The danger here is that those making pronouncements assume an aura of infallibility, stemming from their certainty about the correctness of their interpretations and conclusions. But do evangelicals who agree on the basic tenets of the faith have to agree on complex contemporary issues?

Pragmatism and compromise

Attitudes differ over the extent to which we should be pragmatic in arriving at decisions, and these differences may lead to conflict.

> Let's imagine a young couple, David and Suzanne. They don't normally buy raffle tickets, because they consider them a form of gambling. On one occasion, though, they are approached by a neighbour's child to buy some tickets for a cause that means a great deal to them. Since they consider it worthy of support, and since they don't see how they can support it by a routine donation, they break their principle and buy a book of tickets. They could have clung to their principles, and refused to purchase any tickets. In this instance, therefore, they have acted as pragmatists, and have veered from their ideal.

> Let's now imagine another scenario. Another couple, Jim and Leanne, have a ten-year-old son, Chris, who plays soccer at a local junior soccer club. The games are nor-

mally played on Saturdays, although occasionally there are special tournaments on Sunday mornings. Jim and Leanne are opposed to Sunday sport and don't allow Chris to play any of the Sunday games. This is accepted by all concerned, except on one occasion when it proves impossible to make up a full team. Chris is desperately needed, and he could play and still attend church. However, Jim and Leanne consider this would be a compromise which must be resisted. They are not pragmatists and are prepared to put up with whatever criticism may arise.

In both illustrations the couples want to live by an ideal; one couple is prepared to fall short of this in order to accomplish something they consider worthwhile, but the other couple clings to the ideal. David and Suzanne acted as pragmatists, albeit reluctantly. Jim and Leanne refused to do so. For David and Suzanne pragmatic considerations may sometimes have a part to play in their decisions, although always against a background of clearly-defined principles and guidelines. By contrast, Jim and Leanne are unwilling to be pragmatists under any circumstances. For them, there is only one guide, the 'ideal' or the 'absolute'; pragmatism is always compromise, and compromise is always to be shunned.

Many Christians are only prepared to live by one of these approaches, not both. They see them as alternatives, even as mutually exclusive. Whenever this happens, it results in one of two extremes: legalism or libertarianism, absolute rules or no rules at all. I reject this 'either/or' answer; for me, the two approaches, and the two sets of theological truths are complementary, and both are essential in order to function as a Christian in a secular society.

It is also vital to recognize the place of both approaches if controversy is to be coped with. As long as only one of these approaches is accepted, controversy is unavoidable. Whenever the ideal comes up against the pragmatic, there is no way forward. And it is more pertinent in Christian circles than in secular ones, because in Christian circles the pragmatic is readily associated with compromise, and compromise is regarded as an evil.

This, however, is an illusion, as demonstrated by an issue such as divorce. The ideal is life-long marriage, but this is frequently not adhered to even in Christian circles. Christians are divorced and remarry. This may be substandard in terms of biblical ideals, and of the explicit teaching of Christ, and yet Christian communities accommodate the existence of divorced Christians in their midst. In addition, since many divorced people are converted and become part of Christian communities, their needs and expectations have to be accommodated.

I can envisage a church community excluding divorced Christians on the ground that they have failed to live up to 'what-ought-to-be'. In practice, however, such communities appear to be rare. Rather, we live with the reality of 'what-is', and it forms the basis of much pastoral and counselling assistance for divorced people. Whatever one's own position on divorce and remarriage, Christian love and concern have to be demonstrated to those who are divorced. In other words, pastoral concerns demand an acceptance of the reality of divorce — even within Christian circles. To acknowledge the 'what-is', is simply the beginning of a Christian approach to those in need of understanding and love. It need not weaken the biblical ideal. There is no incompatibility between the two.

Public policy

Christians differ over the extent to which they consider Christian values should be adopted by society or should be imposed on society. For some Christians no distinction is made between Christian values and society's values; whatever is regarded as the ideal or norm within a Christian framework is also regarded as the only acceptable norm for a pluralist society. Consequently, they advocate their own standards, and nothing less, for society, even if these standards have to be forced upon it. Other Christians recognize that, however much they might wish to see Christian standards adopted by society, they can neither impose these on society nor expect society to adopt them in their entirety.

These two approaches to the relationship between Christian ethical standards and those of society result in different social policies. The first group of Christians accepts nothing less than Christian standards for society. Consequently, if Christians within this group reject artificial donor insemination (DI) as an ethically acceptable practice for Christians, they refuse to accept that DI should be permissible within society. It follows from this that some of these Christians advocate making DI a criminal offence. Other Christians recognize that, even if they personally find DI ethically unacceptable, DI may be a legitimate procedure within society as a whole. What these Christians will do is attempt to find ways of regulating DI so that the interests of the parties involved, especially of the children, are given considerable protection.

In other words, even though these two groups of Christians agree on the ethical issues involved, their views on public policy are different. Not only this, but each group's views are open to considerable misunderstanding by the other group, and hence controversy may ensue.

What this demonstrates is that Christians may come into conflict with one another, even when their views on a social issue are identical. The same holds true for various theological issues — attitudes towards homosexuality is one. Conflict arises over differences in the extent to which Christians consider their perspectives should be inculcated upon others within society. Is one or other approach more in accordance with biblical teaching?

There are a number of levels at which ethical debate has to be conducted. There is the Christian level, at which one can assume a general acceptance of the same basic ethical principles. Even here, though, there is frequent disagreement concerning the specific applications of some principles. Nevertheless, discussion can take place within a more or less agreed framework which constitutes the basis for advice and assistance. Beyond it are other levels, depending on the degree of acceptance of Christian or other presuppositions. At these levels, recommendations for society will represent a compromise between what Christians advocate as Christian action, and what they find society will be prepared to accept.

According to this approach, the Christian contribution is an attempt to influence society's thinking and attitudes as much as possible, so that decisions and trends within society will be influenced by this contribution. In other words, the final outcome for society will be different from the outcome that would have occurred apart from the Christian influence. But in order to do this, certain procedures or social arrangements within society may have to be tolerated in terms of public policy, even if they are substandard in Christian ethical terms. Such tolerance does not denote acceptance of these procedures or arrangements, but is simply a realistic appraisal of what modifications may be possible to bring about. This, in turn, accepts the legitimacy of dialogue between Christians and those of other theological and philosophical persuasions, and also of the active and positive involvement of Christians within society.

This committee-approach to public policy is a positive one, even if it lacks the opposition front of those who stand back from society and remorselessly attack its standards. Unfortunately, it is also another source of division within Christian circles, since those who appear to give way to secular standards are sometimes regarded as betraying the faith.

The crucial issue for Christians is the extent to which

we are prepared to accept the integrity of those adopting a different approach from ours. If we insist that any approach other than ours signifies lack of integrity and lack of true faith, fragmentation of the body of Christ is inevitable.

Evangelicals and society

Why do evangelicals differ on important issues within contemporary society? The first and obvious answer is that there are legitimate differences in biblical interpretation, but this is not all. There are personality differences and a diverse range of past experiences, both of which colour our responses, even as Christians.

When confronted by new experiences or developments (whether in biomedical technology or styles of church worship) we show a range of responses. For example, an immediate response for many is an *innate response*, and frequently this is one of alarm. The developments (whatever they may be) and their ramifications are beyond our comprehension, and we wish they were not occurring. They represent new and forbidding territory, and our innate response is to throw up our hands in horror. This may be no more than an initial reaction, and on reflection we may begin to place the nature and implications of the developments in perspective. Nevertheless, the innate response is not to be ignored, although in its unformulated state it may not represent an adequate Christian response.

Closely associated with an innate response, is a *conservative response*. This tends to be one of rejection. We may vehemently oppose developments which appear to reject all we stand for. They represent change and new directions, introducing new dilemmas and new prospects with their questioning of existing ethical and professional (or perhaps liturgical) frameworks.

The complete antithesis is a *liberal response*. We may wholeheartedly welcome new developments, since, by definition, anything new is automatically better than that which at present exists. Such developments may also be seen as ushering in a better world, in that they represent an overthrow of present standards and expectations.

In contrast to these approaches, a fourth response is a *dispassionate, critical response*. According to this, the developments in question will be analysed, and an attempt made to assess the reasons for the alarm and the nature of the hope they appear to offer. Questions are asked, such as whether these developments are as good as some people claim, whether they offer as much hope as some are suggesting, whether they are dangerous in some regards, and whether they may be misleading for some people.

Responses will always fall within this range; and it applies to Christians as well as others. Some get no further than an innate response, with its tendency towards automatic rejection of new developments. Some always go for new things, whether they be new cars, new clothes, new technologies, or new beliefs; others are the exact opposite. Not surprisingly, therefore, if Christians are being governed by any of the first three responses, their attitudes will reflect the culture and environment in which they live. By contrast, the critical approach has more to commend it, but even it will not ensure that criticism is truly being undertaken along Christian lines.

The challenge for Christians is to go beyond all of these responses. No matter what their initial response, Christians have to determine whether their attitudes are informed by biblically-based principles and theological thinking. It's of major importance to recognize one's personal preferences, and then to assess whether these are being governed by truly Christian thinking. The crucial issue for Christians is whether they are *responding Christianly* to the plethora of developments that are radically transforming the face of contemporary life. If we fail to go this far in our thinking, we will find

ourselves at loggerheads with others, including other
Christians, for no better reason than personality differences. The temptation, then, is to dress up these differences in theological garb. It is a tragic situation and one
that brings no glory to God.

Even when we have struggled to assess issues Christianly, we shall still find we have our disagreements.
But, at least, we should know precisely *why* we disagree,
and the reasons underlying this disagreement are then
amenable to discussion and serious debate. Without the
benefits of such an assessment, we have nowhere from
which to start, and the situation is ripe for profitless and
destructive controversy. It is to this type of assessment
that we now turn.

Questions for group discussion

1. What do you consider as central and peripheral
    issues for Christians? How do you distinguish be-
    tween the two?

2. To what extent do you think evangelical Christians
    have freedom to explore new areas of thought or
    practice? Give examples of what you think might/
    might not be acceptable.

3. What measures do you think should be taken to
    avoid confrontation within churches?

4. 'Compromise' is often regarded as a dirty word,
    since it stands for accepting second-best. Do you
    agree with this, or is it sometimes the path to be
    followed by Christians? Try and think of specific
    examples.

5. If you are faced with a novel way of doing some-
    thing, how do you react? Discuss the various re-
    actions within the group. Think of ways we can
    build on these initial reactions and make them more
    Christian.

FOUR

Judging and Forgiving Others

Destructive criticism

To set the scene, let us imagine the following:

> Whatever you do, don't go to *that* church. The people who go there aren't true Christians. After all, they don't believe in the inerrancy of Scripture or if they do they keep it very quiet. Their pastors never preach on the importance of inerrancy. Neither do they believe in God's absolute sovereignty or in predestination. They allow non-members to take part in the Lord's supper, and they even allow women to preach. People who allow practices like that have been tainted by the world, and are compromising with secularism. They can't be trusted, and you should keep away from them. Our church is different. We make sure that everyone knows where they stand regarding Scripture. Not only does our pastor preach on it regularly, but we have also struck three people off the membership roll because they refused to sign a statement affirming biblical inerrancy. All they do now is to go to some house group, and spend their time singing choruses. That doesn't say much for their Christianity.

This is an illustration of the sort of *destructive criticism* in which Christians all too frequently indulge; it's a

46

criticism of those who don't subscribe to precisely the same beliefs we ourselves hold. There's nothing wrong with a difference of viewpoint on these or many other issues, but when we condemn others for holding contrary beliefs, the end result is division, misunderstanding, and disharmony.

Not only this, but one or two selected beliefs are made into the litmus test of true Christianity. Other aspects of these people's lives or beliefs are not considered. They are condemned because they fail to pass one particular test. Everything else pales beside this and is considered of no value.

Seeing minor faults in others

> Do not judge, or you too will be judged. For in the same way you judge others, you will be judged, and with the measure you use, it will be measured to you.
>
> Why do you look at the speck of sawdust in your brother's eye and pay no attention to the plank in your own eye? How can you say to your brother, 'Let me take the speck out of your eye,' when all the time there is a plank in your own eye? You hypocrite, first take the plank out of your own eye, and then you will see clearly to remove the speck from your brother's eye.
>
> Do not give dogs what is sacred; do not throw your pearls to pigs. If you do, they may trample them under their feet, and then turn and tear you to pieces.
>
> Matthew 7:1–6

Jesus' teaching on hypocrisy, and on the importance of consistency between external appearance and inward reality, is preceded in the Sermon on the Mount (Matthew 7:1, 2) by what appears to be a categorical statement — *under no circumstances are we to judge others*. The reason Jesus gives, is that if we judge others there will be certain consequences: we ourselves will be judged, and this judgement will be based on precisely the same criteria as those we use to judge others. The two sets of criteria are parallel: God will judge us in the same way we judge others; he will apply to us the precise rules we apply to others.

But this isn't all. Jesus goes further, because he is aware of how devious we are. The two sets of criteria are not exactly parallel, because our temptation is to judge a *minor* fault in others while ignoring a *major* fault in our own lives. Whatever faults we may detect in others are likely to be small compared with the faults that characterize us, even if our faults are of a totally different nature from those we vigorously denounce in others. We tend to worry about the speck of dirt in another's eye, but readily ignore the vast log in our own.

We, too, are at fault. However dreadful we think another person is, we ourselves are far from blameless. If this is so, are we in a position to judge others? Not only this, but if we are to be judged along the same lines we use for judging others, shall we not be judged far more harshly than we fondly imagine?

According to Jesus, we are not to set ourselves up as judges of others within the body of Christ, censuring and condemning them. He warns against any form of censoriousness, where our sole interest lies in finding fault with others, destructively condemning them, and repeatedly misinterpreting their motives and actions. In acting like this, we elevate ourselves, becoming judges, and passing sentence on them. It happens when we regard ourselves as superior to those around us, including our fellow Christians. By implication, we downgrade those Christians with whom we disagree, bestowing upon them a status lower than that bestowed upon them by Christ. *We ourselves have become judges*, taking for ourselves a position God has reserved exclusively for himself. The end result is disharmony and disunity, and it is this that tears communities apart.

It doesn't mean we are to suspend our critical faculties. There is still a place for discernment, as long as it is done constructively and positively, realizing that we ourselves may be wrong and may have a great deal to learn. This is clearly brought out when Jesus tells his listeners to remove the speck from the other person's eye *after* they have taken the plank out of their own eye. It may not be easy to remove obstacles in our own lives, and perhaps Jesus didn't expect this to be done. Nevertheless, he was adamant that it had to be accomplished before we are able to see clearly enough to condemn other people. Self-criticism is essential and we must always accept the correction of others.

Jesus had no room for judgementalism for its own sake. Since God alone is the ultimate judge, judgement is his responsibility and not ours. This is not simply a negative stricture; its positive feature is that we have been freed from judging both the motives and actions of others. The realization that we are to leave this in God's hands is profoundly liberating.

But what, we may ask, about Jesus himself? He was ruthless in his criticism of the Pharisees. Was he inconsistent? Perhaps, after all, it is impossible to live by the standards apparently laid down in this passage. Does it mean we are never to open our mouths, no matter how other people live or what they believe? Are we to allow anything and everything to pass by without a murmur? To answer these questions, we have to move on and see Jesus in a different context, where his emphases were rather different.

Hypocrisy

Then Jesus said to the crowds and to his disciples: "The teachers of the law and the Pharisees sit in Moses' seat. So you must obey them and do everything they tell you. But do not do what they do, for they do not practise what they preach. They tie up heavy loads and put them on men's shoulders, but they themselves are not willing to lift a finger to move them.

"Everything they do is done for men to see: They make their phylacteries wide and the tassels on their garments long; they love the place of honour at banquets and the most important seats in the synagogues; they love to be greeted in the market-places and to have men call them 'Rabbi'.

"But you are not to be called 'Rabbi', for you have only one Master and you are all brothers. And do not call anyone on earth 'father' for you have one Father, and he is in heaven. Nor are you to be called 'teacher', for you have one Teacher, the Christ. The greatest among you will be your servant. For whoever exalts himself will be humbled, and whoever humbles himself will be exalted. . . .

"Woe to you, teachers of the law and Pharisees, you hypocrites! You give a tenth of your spices — mint, dill and cummin. But you have neglected the more important matters of the law — justice, mercy and faithfulness. You should have practised the latter, without neglecting the former. You blind guides! You strain out a gnat but swallow a camel.

"Woe to you, teachers of the law and Pharisees, you hypocrites! You clean the outside of the cup and dish, but inside they are full of greed and self-indulgence. Blind Pharisee! First clean the inside of the cup and dish, and then the outside also will be clean.

"Woe to you, teachers of the law and Pharisees, you hypocrites! You are like whitewashed tombs, which look beautiful on the outside but on the inside are full of dead men's bones and everything unclean. In the same way, on the outside you appear to people as righteous but on the inside you are full of hypocrisy and wickedness. . . .

"You snakes! You brood of vipers! How will you escape being condemned to hell?"

                                        Matthew 23:1–12, 23–28, 33

Jesus assailed the Pharisees in the harshest of terms, calling them hypocrites, describing them as blind guides and blind fools, likening them to whitewashed tombs, and calling them snakes and sons of snakes. Not unnaturally we might ask whether this doesn't justify our condemning people, including other Christians, when we consider they are in the wrong or are leading others astray. Let's look more closely at the nature of Jesus' criticism.

The condemnation is of the *hypocrisy of the Pharisees*. They were the religious leaders of the people, the ones to provide direction on all spiritual matters, and yet they repeatedly *said* one thing and *did* something else. Their responsibility was to act as the interpreters of the law of Moses, and yet Jesus quite specifically told the people to obey what the Pharisees said but *under no circumstances to imitate their actions*. The reason for this was the gaping chasm between that which they taught and that which they lived out. Having imposed vast legal burdens on the people, they did nothing to help them carry the load. They flaunted their authority, and appeared strikingly religious. They had the best seats at feasts and reserved seats in the synagogues, and they encouraged people to call them 'teacher'. Alongside this show and ostentation went an abysmal failure to live up to the standards they set for others.

They were reminiscent of a person today who emphasizes in church the central importance of honesty and integrity, but whose management of his factory is known for its deceit and dishonesty. When preaching on honesty and uprightness is accompanied by a life of shady dealings and the exploitation of others, the contrast is devastating. By acting out a part, such a person would quite rightly be regarded as one of the hypocrites of society. So with the Pharisees; they too acted out a part and were the hypocrites of their society. These were the people who made a great show of their religion, whether it was their giving to those in need, their public praying, or their fasting (Matt. 6). It was done to demonstrate how religious they were; their only reward was the praise of others.

What Jesus did in Matthew 23, was to condem hypocrisy of this type rather than the individuals. He was upset by the glaring gulf between what the Pharisees wished people to believe they were, and what they actually were. It was a deliberate living out of a lie. It was like a pastor who tells his congregation to 'give sacrificially to the Lord's work', and then pockets a significant proportion of that money for himself, enabling him to live at a much higher standard than those in his congregation. Or, like the Christian leader who lays down a stringent moral code for his followers, castigating all who fail to live up to it, while he himself makes no attempt to live by the same code. It is this *calibre of hypocrisy* that is condemned by Jesus.

When confronted by the Pharisees, Jesus was confronted by those in positions of leadership who were flagrantly hypocritical, saying one thing and knowingly doing the direct opposite. What appalled Jesus was the hypocrisy of those who should have known better and yet were deliberately leading people astray by their double standards. By contrast, the judgement Jesus outlawed in Matthew 7 is the vindictive condemnation of our contemporaries, something in which we're not to indulge at any cost.

Jesus did not condemn the Pharisees as individuals. He condemned them as a group for their blatant two-faced lifestyle rather than for their erroneous beliefs. It is hypocrisy of this magnitude that is by far the greatest enemy of true Christianity, and we should be aware of the immense dangers of such hypocrisy. This is not the failure of someone, even a Christian leader, who commits sin or falls from grace. The failure here involves a wholesale duplicity of standards.

Repeatedly, the Pharisees emphasized the minutiae of the law while overlooking important emphases such as justice, mercy, and honesty. Jesus pictured them looking at their drink and longing to get rid of the fly in it, while at the same time failing to notice that they were actually swallowing a camel. It's a bit like us, inordinately concerned about the way people dress in church, while failing to treat them as human beings made in the image of God. Or, emphasizing the method of baptism, while forgetting what it means in terms of God's forgiveness and redemption.

The Pharisees were characterized by their concern with appearances, so much so that they overlooked something of far greater importance — what they were like as people. They made sure the outside of the cup was clean but didn't bother with the inside, with their violence and selfishness. And in the most damning of all Jesus' pictures he depicted them as whitewashed tombs; they looked respectable, but in reality were nothing more than bones and decaying corpses. There could be no more vivid portrayal of hypocrisy than this, with its overtones of death and decay.

It highlights why we are not to judge individuals along the lines of Matthew 7. That sort of judgement is most easily made by hypocrites, by those who pretend to be one thing and yet deep down are something else. It is easy for those who are not particularly concerned about consistency between their beliefs and actions to pick holes in others and point out where they are going wrong. On the other hand, this type of judgement is far more difficult for those who are aware of their own sinfulness and of their own pitiful lack of consistency.

False prophets and false teaching

Jesus talked about false prophets and false teaching. In talking about *false prophets* (Matt. 7:15–20), Jesus emphasized the contrast between appearances and reality. The people Jesus described as false prophets looked like genuine prophets. But their outward appearance was deceptive, since instead of protecting and building up, they destroyed. They looked like sheep, yet they were wolves. Using this illustration Jesus warned his hearers to look closely at what people *do*, and not listen simply to the palatable words they utter. This is the deception of hypocrisy. While we are to refrain from judging others, we are to be on our guard against hypocrisy; it is this, more than anything else, that destroys true Christianity.

As far as Jesus was concerned, hypocrisy was the main danger, but it wasn't all. There was also *false teaching* (Matt. 5:17–48; 15:1–9), another failing of the Pharisees who manipulated the teaching of the Mosaic law for their own ends. They misunderstood important elements of the law and so reduced its implications for ordinary people and for society. The result was that they reduced its spiritual and moral impact. By emphasizing the external and the obvious, they missed the essence of the law. In an attempt to make the law serve their own purposes, they missed its profundity and revolutionary character.

What is to be criticized is any trend that diminishes the impact of the gospel. The nature of the trend is irrelevant; it may be some theological emphasis that detracts from the person and work of Christ; it may be dead orthodoxy where Christ is central but all spiritual life seems to be extinguished; or it may be any particular belief, spiritual gift, or social concern that threatens the centrality of Christ.

This *is* rightfully our concern, and yet even this needs to be seen as subsidiary to the detrimental nature of hypocrisy. Jesus had far more to say about hypocrisy than he did about theological orthodoxy. The ultimate test is always whether it will bring glory to God or whether it will detract from bringing glory to God. There is no doubt that any teaching that denies the centrality of Christ as Saviour and Lord, detracts from God'd glory. But, so does hypocrisy. We have to be exceedingly careful in our criticism of others since we ourselves may be far from blameless, while our enthusiasm to condemn false doctrine may itself detract from the centrality of Christ.

There is a place for criticism of the beliefs of other Christians, since Jesus did this with regard to the Pharisees. But we must always remember that God is the ultimate judge, and we are all responsible before him for our beliefs and actions (Matt. 12:33–37). Also, as Jesus

demonstrated in the parable of the weeds (Matt. 13:
24–30), responsibility for pulling up the weeds, that is,
for removing unbelievers and hypocrites from the
church, belongs to God and not to us. The temptation to
step in prematurely and do this ourselves is a very great
one. It is so great, that it is sometimes regarded as a sign
of faithfulness to God. To be faithful is to be vigilant in
keeping the church pure. The difficulty is that we lack a
consensus regarding what constitutes purity, especially
when purity of doctrine is being considered. The parable
of the weeds is a gentle reminder that God himself will
remove the weeds in his own time. *Our* primary concern
is to deal with the *quality* of our lives.

Discernment

We have to be extremely careful in our condemnation of
others. Nevertheless, there is room for positive and
constructive approaches, and this is where *discernment*
comes in. When others aimed to trip up Jesus with trick
questions, he dealt positively with them. Time and again
he turned criticism of either himself or his disciples into
something helpful. When the Pharisees attempted to
trap him over the paying of taxes, he took them seriously and provided clear directions about their respective obligations to the emperor and to God (Matt.
22:15–22). This wasn't what they had expected, but
Jesus' refusal to deride them, opened up an important
avenue for him to show them their obligations within
society.

Similarly, when the Sadducees thought they had Jesus
trapped with their story of the seven brothers and one
widow, Jesus again took them seriously and turned their
trick question into positive teaching on the resurrection
(Matthew 22:23–33). It would have been very easy for
Jesus to condemn their trickery and false belief. Had he
done that, the end result would have been entirely

negative. Instead, he was able to use the opportunity his adversaries had given him to address their unbelief. Instead of simply winning a confrontational battle, Jesus spoke directly to them as people, and to their needs and lack of faith.

A somewhat different incident that Jesus treated in a similar fashion was that of his dealings with the woman at Bethany who anointed him with expensive perfume (Matt. 26:6–13). When the disciples saw what was happening they became angry at the waste. By contrast, Jesus recognized the positive elements in this act and emphasized not its waste, but its beauty and possible significance. Instead of being judgemental, he was discerning and sympathetic.

This is an emphasis all Christians should take seriously. We are not to act as judges, but we do have the opportunity to encourage others, moving alongside them in an attempt to get them to reassess the implications of their thinking, and to turn even criticism into positive instruction. Even when it comes to strong disagreements with others or explicit sin within the Christian community, the issue is to be talked through, others are to be involved as go-betweens, and everything possible is to be done to resolve the disagreement or hurt before bringing it into the open before the community at large (Matt. 18:15–17). This emphasizes the importance of dialogue and discussion, as opposed to judgement and condemnation.

It is the only way that recognizes our equality in Christ and our oneness in the body of Christ. Harsh and precipitate judgement is one of the surest ways of ruining the work of Christ; it is also an appalling witness to outsiders. If there is to be one major difference between Christians and non-Christians, it is to be in the way we handle the differences that inevitably occur among us. Judgement and hypocrisy are to be replaced by discernment, taking other believers and their viewpoints seriously, and disagreeing in a positive spirit.

Taking account of the weak

Now consider some of Paul's teaching.

Accept him whose faith is weak, without passing judgment on disputable matters. One man's faith allows him to eat everything, but another man, whose faith is weak, eats only vegetables. The man who eats everything must not look down on him who does not, and the man who does not eat everything must not condemn the man who does, for God has accepted him. Who are you to judge someone else's servant? To his own master he stands or falls. And he will stand, for the Lord is able to make him stand.

One man considers one day more sacred than another; another man considers every day alike. Each one should be fully convinced in his own mind. He who regards one day as special, does so to the Lord. He who eats meat, eats to the Lord, for he gives thanks to God; and he who abstains, does so to the Lord and gives thanks to God. For none of us lives to himself alone and none of us dies to himself alone. If we live, we live to the Lord; and if we die, we die to the Lord. So, whether we live or die, we belong to the Lord.

For this very reason, Christ died and returned to life so that he might be the Lord of both the dead and the living. You then, why do you judge your brother? Or why do you look down on your brother? For we will all stand before God's judgment seat. . . .

Therefore let us stop passing judgment on one another. Instead, make up your mind not to put any stumbling-block or obstacle in your brother's way. As one who is in the Lord Jesus I am fully convinced that no food is unclean in itself. But if anyone regards something as unclean, then for him it is unclean. If your brother is distressed because of what you eat, you are no longer acting in love. Do not by your eating destroy your brother for whom Christ died. Do not allow what you consider good to be spoken of as evil. For the kingdom of God is not a matter of eating and drinking, but of righteousness, peace and joy in the Holy Spirit, because anyone who serves Christ in this way is pleasing to God and approved by men.

Let us therefore make every effort to do what leads to peace and to mutual edification. Do not destroy the work of God for the sake of food. All food is clean, but it is wrong for a man to eat anything that causes someone else to stumble. It is better not to eat meat or drink wine or to do anything else that will cause your brother to fall.

So whatever you believe about these things keep between yourself and God. Blessed is the man who does not condemn himself by what he approves. But the man who has doubts is condemned if he eats, because his eating is not from faith; and everything that does not come from faith is sin.

We who are strong ought to bear with the failings of the weak and not to please ourselves. Each of us should please his neighbour for his good, to build him up.

Romans 14:1–10, 13–22; 15:1, 2

The core of Paul's arguments here centres on 'disputable matters', peripheral or secondary matters, that are not central to the faith. They are matters on which different Christians have different perspectives; they are open to dispute. The disputable matters with which Paul was concerned as he wrote to the Christians in Rome, were what should or should not be eaten, and whether some days were or were not to be regarded as sacred.

On these questions there were different viewpoints within the church. Some, whom Paul termed 'weak', would not eat certain foods. Those Christians who felt no such constraints tended to look down on their 'weaker' brethren, whereas those who had these constraints condemned the ones who ate everything. There was condemnation and judgement on both sides; to each group only their own position was 'correct'.

For Paul it was not a question of right and wrong, correct and incorrect; neither group had the authority to judge the other. All that mattered was the relationship each group had with the Lord: 'To his own master he stands or falls'. These were disputable matters, and what was of crucial importance was that these people stood firm as Christians, something that depended on the Lord — not on their 'correctness' or otherwise in relation to some arbitrary issues.

Paul's approach was entirely different from theirs. He was not judgemental; the issues were too insignificant for that. The important issue was one of commitment. They were to give thanks to God for everything. Some would give thanks for a special day, others would give thanks for the meat they were eating, and yet others would give thanks because they were abstaining from eating meat. Since the particular action was relatively unimportant, Paul showed little concern that diametrically opposite practices existed within the same Christian community.

What Paul saw as crucial, was that all lived 'to the Lord'. But failure to live like this was of concern since it led to judgementalism, looking down on others, treating them in ways unlike those of Christ who died and rose for them. In the end, all have to give an account of themselves, their actions and their motives, before God.

As if his arguments had not already been clear enough, Paul tells his followers to stop passing judgement on one another. It's as if this simple restraint was too difficult for most of them, as it is too difficult for most of us. He underlines the point that judging others over disputable matters places stumbling-blocks in the way of those who are being judged. Our tendency is to argue that incorrect beliefs, even over disputable and peripheral issues, are a danger to the spiritual welfare of Christians and we feel a need to 'put them right'. Paul's approach is quite different. He sees harsh judgementalism as the obstacle, because different perspectives on these unclear issues are of no significance. Differences of this nature don't pose great obstacles to anyone's spiritual welfare.

Paul goes further than this. You may think he was agnostic over these marginal matters, but he wasn't. Far from it: he knows what he thinks about eating food, even food offered to idols. For him, no food is unclean. He has taken sides, and yet he still respects those who adopt the opposite position and who regard some food as unclean and, therefore, not to be eaten. Paul accepts that for them to eat such food when they are convinced it is unclean, would be wrong. He respects their integrity and refuses to criticize them.

Not only this; it has implications for his own behaviour. If he knows that his eating certain food would distress a fellow Christian, he refrains from doing so in their company. He hasn't just refused to condemn them, he has even taken account of their viewpoint in modifying his own behaviour. Why? Because what is of supreme importance is their spiritual welfare and not a particular viewpoint on a disputable matter. Love is supreme; judgementalism and winning arguments have no place in the lives of Christians.

The implications of our actions on fellow-Christians are relevant when deciding how to respond to differences of opinion within the body of Christ. Even if we consider our position to be the correct one, and the best one for the church, we must ensure that what we consider to be good is not interpreted by others as evil. This can easily happen when our critical attitudes overwhelm the correctness of our position.

We need to ask ourselves repeatedly what influence our attitudes and demeanour have on others. To destroy another Christian because of what we perceive to be the rightness of our position on a disputable matter, should be unthinkable; yet it happens. The reason it is unthinkable is, as Paul phrases it, because the kingdom of God is concerned with righteousness, peace and joy in the Holy Spirit, and not with issues such as what we eat and drink. It is not concerned with disputable and peripheral matters. Our concern is to serve Christ and to please God, and this is not accomplished by winning battles over peripheral matters, regardless of how important we consider these matters to be.

Sacrificing precision on peripheral matters

Paul hammers home these critical concepts: the work of God is not to be destroyed for the sake of food (or our favourite debating topics); we are to do nothing in these matters that will cause another person to stumble; we are, even, to refrain from doing something wholesome if that might cause other believers to take their eyes off Christ. The governing principle in all we do should be to strengthen others in their faith, uphold them, and bring them peace.

Battles may well have to be fought over central issues, those that provide the skeleton of true biblical Christianity. When issues such as these are lost, people's relationship to Christ is placed in jeopardy. However, battles over disputable and peripheral matters lead in the opposite direction — it is the battles themselves that jeopardize people's relationship to Christ. Paul goes so far as to comment that there are situations where we are to keep quiet about our beliefs on some peripheral matters, since these may hinder fellow Christians. Consider the following situation.

John is well-known in local church circles for his advocacy of female leadership within the church. He does everything he can to ensure that women are provided with opportunities for exercising their spiritual gifts. The church of which he is senior pastor has women elders, church services are frequently led by women, and women preach relatively frequently. He would like this to be the pattern in all churches throughout the denomination to which he belongs. However, when it comes to discussions with other local clergy, he frequently says relatively little about women in leadership — not because he lacks commitment to this cause, but because he knows it would prove intensely divisive in this particular situation. He considers that work on forwarding the gospel in the community is of supreme importance, whereas bitter controversy over this issue — important as he considers it to be — would simply stifle any joint evangelistic initiatives among all the churches.

The principle guiding John, and one to which we are to adhere, is that we are to support and assist those who are weaker in the faith than we are (they may not accept this designation, but that is beside the point!). Those with whom we have dealings are to be built up in all crucial matters, and we are to live for them. In order to accomplish this, precision on peripheral matters may, on some occasions, have to be sacrificed.

Extent of God's forgiveness

At that time the disciples came to Jesus and asked, "Who is the greatest in the kingdom of heaven?"

He called a little child and had him stand among them. And he said: "I tell you the truth, unless you change and become like little children, you will never enter the kingdom of heaven. Therefore, whoever humbles himself like this child is the greatest in the kingdom of heaven. And whoever welcomes a little child like this in my name welcomes me. . . .

"See that you do not look down on one of these little ones. For I tell you that their angels in heaven always see the face of my Father in heaven.

"What do you think? If a man owns a hundred sheep, and one of them wanders away, will he not leave the ninety-nine on the hills and go to look for the one that wandered off? And if he finds it, I tell you the truth, he is happier about that one sheep than about the ninety-nine that did not wander off. In the same way your Father in heaven is not willing that any of these little ones should be lost."

Matthew 18:1–5, 10–14

Who is going to be the most successful? Who is going to get to the top? To this question Jesus gave his disciples one of his totally unexpected replies: the greatest in the kingdom of heaven is a child; the greatest is the weakest, the most vulnerable, the frailest, the least pretentious, the most humble.

To enter the kingdom of heaven, one must become

like a little child — accepting, straightforward, innocent, guileless. Not only this, but one must protect children and look after their welfare as part of the more general principle of protecting the weak and defenceless. In the eyes of Jesus this is an obligation from which there is no escape. We are not to despise or lead astray a single one of them.

But why treat the weak and defenceless like this? Why not trample them into the ground, exploit them and use them for our own purposes? The answer appears to be that we are to care for them because this is in accordance with God's own priorities, stemming, as it does, from his commitment to his creation and from his desire that all should be able to develop into mature, responsible human beings.

To illustrate the extent of this commitment Jesus tells a parable. Out of a hundred sheep, one is lost; ninety-nine are safe. In most societies many people would be more than happy with a 99 per cent return; after all one per cent is hardly very much. It could have been infinitely worse; only sixty or seventy might have returned. But ninety-nine have come back. Shouldn't the man in the parable have been very grateful that only one was lost? Most people would tend to emphasize the ninety-nine that were safe; and yet God's priorities emphasize the one that was lost — the one that didn't make it, the one that fell by the wayside. It's not that the ninety-nine safe ones didn't matter; but the loss of even one was considered a catastrophe.

The sheep in the parable are all in need of protection and guidance. No indication is given of their state of health, the quality of their wool, or their market value. We are not led to believe that the one that was lost was a prize sheep or an impoverished, pathetic one. We have no idea why this particular one wandered off; and in terms of the thrust of the parable all such considerations are irrelevant. It was simply that one of the sheep was lost, and, if at all possible, had to be saved.

And this is what God's forgiveness is all about. His concern is for all, whoever they are, whatever their merits or lack of merits. God's love is indiscriminate; it refuses to choose because it is always seeking the recalcitrant one per cent.

Forgiveness within the Christian community

"If your brother sins against you, go and show him his fault, just between the two of you. If he listens to you, you have won your brother over. But if he will not listen, take one or two others along, so that 'every matter may be established by the testimony of two or three witnesses.' If he refuses to listen to them, tell it to the church; and if he refuses to listen even to the church, treat him as you would a pagan or a tax collector. . . .

"Again, I tell you that if two of you on earth agree about anything you ask for, it will be done for you by my Father in heaven. For where two or three come together in my name, there am I with them."

Matthew 18:15–17, 19, 20

God's forgiveness is the base from which everything begins. But how does forgiveness operate in the ordinariness of day-to-day existence? God forgave us, and we are to forgive others.

Whatever our ideals may be, we fail to live up to them. We fall into sin, and sometimes we are wrong. We may be wrong because we have no desire to understand a situation, don't have all the facts, or simply have made a mistake. Inevitably, therefore, there will be disagreement between the followers of Christ. When we fail to understand an issue or each other, or resolutely adhere to our own position regardless of the evidence, difficulties ensue and forgiveness is required.

But how do we forgive others? Jesus was well aware of these practical difficulties, and so he tells another story — about a brother (or sister) who sins against us. We are not told what he had done, whether it was what we might (inaccurately) refer to as a big sin or a little sin; whether it was a major moral catastrophe or something little more than an injudicious way of handling a personality clash. We don't know, and surprisingly, it's irrelevant.

But how can it be irrelevant — a major moral downfall is light-years away from a clash of personalities? In one sense, yes, but in another sense, no. When dealing with forgiveness, the fact that we have to be prepared to forgive another person and the way in which we go about it, are the same regardless of the nature of the sin.

In the parable a brother has sinned, although it is not clear whether it was against us. What do we do? Do we make sure that everyone knows the heinousness of his sin; do we let the whole church know, so that we can get rid of him as quickly as possible, or at least make sure he is disciplined by the elders? If he is in full-time Christian work, do we do our best to get him dismissed from his position, even if he has already repented?

Jesus made a number of suggestions. First, keep it private. Whatever it is, speak to the persons in question, raise the matter troubling you, discuss it, get their side of the matter. Be open to what they have to say. After all, you may have wronged them; you may have misinterpreted their actions or their words; you yourself may be partly to blame. Whatever the situation is, be open to discussion and dialogue. Sometimes, of course, it may not be possible to speak to these persons. Then it may be appropriate to write to them. What is crucial, though, is that there is this person-to-person, quiet, private approach at first. Many of our difficulties in dealing with others could be quickly sorted out if we took this as our first response. However, we can only do it if we are prepared to forgive the others. We also need to bear in mind that *we* may be in the wrong; *we* may be approached to change *our* lifestyle or attitudes.

Unfortunately, this first step in reconciliation may not work. We may be rebuffed; the other persons may not be interested in talking to us, or they may totally reject even the possibility of any error on their part. Then comes the second step: take one or two others along, and discuss the matter while they act as witnesses and arbitrators. Depending on the circumstances, these may be elders or leaders of the church, they may be friends who are respected by both parties, or they may be outside arbitrators from the wider Christian community. More specifically, these others should be leaders in the Christian community or, at least, people who are respected by those within the community. If such leaders are not prepared to back us up, the matter should be laid to rest. There are never to be personal vendettas within the body of Christ — the only reason for approaching fellow-Christians whom we think have erred is to attempt to assist them. Bringing in other responsible and respected Christians is what we might refer to as group consultation, and is the next level at which debate is to take place. When Paul confronted the warring Euodia and Syntyche, he pleaded with them to agree with each other in the Lord, and he asked one of the church leaders to help heal the rift between them (Phil. 4:2,3).

The matter is still relatively private; it is confidential, and the aim of this meeting is to bring reconciliation or repentance. The underlying motive is forgiveness. It is never vindictiveness, pious indignation, or moral superiority. The aim is to bring wholeness and harmony within the Christian community, and to individuals within that community. Repentance may certainly be required, and perhaps not just on the part of the person who has ostensibly sinned; many may have fallen short, and many may have to admit this. But most of it can be done in confidence, and forgiveness always desires this.

Sometimes both approaches fail and it is then, and only then, that the matter is brought out into the open, and the church or the wider Christian community is informed. This is when the debate becomes public, and occurs out in the open. Even at this level, though, there is to be discussion. If the general opinion of the church is that these fellow Christians are at fault, and if they refuse to repent or change their views, they may then be considered as having placed themselves outside the fellowship. In similar vein, when there are issues of disagreement within evangelicalism, church leaders should be brought together to discuss matters and to engage in serious dialogue. There needs to be considerable agreement at this level, before a person or viewpoint is condemned as being outside evangelicalism.

This was the function of the Church Councils in the early years of the church, as with the Council at Jerusalem (Acts 15). In that instance, Paul and Barnabas disagreed sharply with some others in the church on the place of circumcision. As a result they, with some other Christians, went to Jerusalem to discuss the matter with the apostles and elders. There was dialogue and ardent debate, as a result of which agreement was reached. Subsequently, a course of action was adopted to let other churches know about the decisions that had been reached.

The aim, even at this late stage, is that forgiveness and reconciliation can occur. The church should provide support and direction, if that is at all possible, because forgiveness always seeks reconciliation. However, if even this fails, there is no more that can be done, and very, very reluctantly they must be regarded as outsiders — that is what they have made themselves to be. No further avenues are open to forgiveness and reconciliation cannot be accomplished — at least, not in the foreseeable future.

These ways of dealing with disagreements all involve discussion and dialogue, commencing at the personal level and working up to public discussion. All are characterized by a desire to find the mind of Christ, and all treat the erring party as a responsible participant. There is never autocratic condemnation. If agreement appears to be impossible, the parties may have to go their separate ways, as happened when Paul and Barnabas disagreed (Acts 15:36–41). But even when this occurs, respect for the other party is essential, with an acknowledgement that, as far as one is aware, the other party is seeking to be faithful to the Lord.

Forgiveness is not a frothy feeling that allows anything to happen and people to get away with sin. Rather, it is the strength to bring people back to wholeness and righteousness, and to build communities of right relationships. It is central to our lives as the people of God.

Jesus reminded his disciples that where two or three agree about something and ask for it in the Father's name, they have Christ in their midst and their request will be answered. This is the antithesis of the disagreement Jesus had previously been considering. Instead of two people at loggerheads, here they are in agreement; instead of pulling in opposite directions, they are supporting and encouraging each other; instead of tearing one another to shreds, they are building each other up under the direction of Christ. In this situation the church experiences the power of forgiveness; in contrast to the earlier picture of a church in disarray, schismatic and impotent.

Extent of our forgiveness

Then Peter came to Jesus and asked, "Lord, how many times shall I forgive my brother when he sins against me? Up to seven times?" Jesus answered, "I tell you, not seven times, but seventy-seven times.

"Therefore, the kingdom of heaven is like a king who wanted to settle accounts with his servants. As he began the settlement, a man who owed him ten thousand talents was brought to him. Since he was not able to pay, the master ordered that he and his wife and his children and all that he had be sold to repay the debt.

"The servant fell on his knees before him. 'Be patient with me,' he begged, 'and I will pay back everything.'

The servant's master took pity on him, cancelled the debt and let him go.

"But when that servant went out, he found one of his fellow-servants who owed him a hundred denarii. He grabbed him and began to choke him. 'Pay back what you owe me!' he demanded.

"His fellow-servant fell to his knees and begged him, 'Be patient with me, and I will pay you back.'

"But he refused. Instead, he went off and had the man thrown into prison until he could pay the debt. When the other servants saw what had happened, they were greatly distressed and went and told their master everything that had happened.

"Then the master called the servant in. 'You wicked servant,' he said, 'I cancelled all that debt of yours because you begged me to. Shouldn't you have had mercy on your fellow-servant just as I had on you?' In anger his master turned him over to the jailers . . . until he should pay back all he owed.

"This is how my heavenly Father will treat each of you unless you forgive your brother from your heart."

Matthew 18:21–35

Peter had a query. When do we stop forgiving? Perhaps, seven times? That sounds generous by most people's standards, where once is too many. But not for Jesus; for him it is seventy-seven times or as some manuscripts have it, seventy times seven, 490 times. Obviously, it doesn't matter; forgiving never stops, even when there is no response from the other party.

We are to continue forgiving because God continues forgiving us. There is no limit to his forgiveness, and there is to be no limit to ours. God's total forgiveness of us demands total forgiveness on our part; no matter how deeply hurt, scarred and wounded we may have been.

To demonstrate this point Jesus tells another story. It is about a king who cancelled the debt of one of his servants, who owed well over a million dollars. The debt was wiped off, an action that was more than the servant had requested. But that wasn't the end of the story.

A fellow-servant had also come off badly, and he owed the forgiven servant a hundred or so dollars. He, too, was in the wrong and not surprisingly he pleaded that his debt should be gradually paid back. Outraged, the forgiven servant completely ignored his own recent experience and showed no mercy of any description; he was ruthless with his debtor. Even the other servants saw the injustice of this and were so upset that they reported him to the king, whose anger resulted in his forgiveness being replaced by justice and condemnation.

It is easy to misunderstand the condemnation that accompanies the king's response in this story and to think that if we are not faithful, God, like a despot, will cut us down and toss us away. But this is to miss something crucial. The point of God's forgiveness is that he wants us to become more like him; he wants us to adopt more of the characteristics of those who have been created in his image and likeness; he wants to eradicate as far as possible the effects of the fall. Redemption enables us to become more like Christ, and this life-long process can only start from God's forgiveness of us.

The clearest distinguishing mark of Christ was his willingness to forgive — everyone, even his enemies. And it is also the clearest distinguishing mark of his followers. To fail to forgive others, or at the very least to fail to begin to appreciate the need to forgive others, is to admit that we know little of the saving work of Christ. Christians have been forgiven an immense amount, and hence are in a position to forgive others in similar fashion. We have been forgiven so that we, in our turn, can demonstrate God's forgiveness to others, and bring wholeness and light to places and people where there is fragmentation and darkness.

This forgiveness applies especially to those within God's kingdom. Such an obvious statement should be unnecessary, but it's not. Forgiveness begins within the family, supremely within the family of God. Unfortunately, we all too often have the characteristics of rival siblings and not of loving family members. To use another analogy, we are like football teams from neighbouring cities or counties. Friendly rivalry is often replaced by bitter animosity, when all that unites turns to detestation and hatred — they are too much in common. Or, like a political party unable to agree on a favourite strand of party policy, the opposing groups are so alike that they see each small difference as ultimate disloyalty and treachery.

Christians, united on so much, can turn into bitter rivals when a cherished secondary belief is challenged by another Christian. It's then that forgiveness is needed. Those able to forgive their brothers and sisters in the Lord, in the face of failure to agree at some apparently crucial point, are those who have understood the depths and height of forgiveness. Those who stand aloof in these circumstances have failed to take Jesus' teaching to heart.

Forgiveness and controversy

Forgiveness and controversy are rarely dealt with together. However, when looked at in this way, two important perspectives emerge: forgiveness is an essential element in coping with controversy, and forgiveness may prevent controversy.

The first of these perspectives has come through clearly in the preceding pages. No matter what the nature of the controversy, it would be surprising if forgiveness had no part to play. Some think that when controversy results from a difference of opinion on some doctrinal or social policy matter, forgiveness is irrelevant. It doesn't enter the picture. One position is to be advocated, and the other rejected. It may even be expressed in specific Christian terms: one position is the biblical position, and the other is unbiblical. The former is the only position faithful Christians can possibly hold,

and so anyone not subscribing to this position is unfaithful. Why bring forgiveness into such a clear-cut
situation?

I have to admit that, put like this, the case appears a
convincing one. But it is deceptive, for it is only this
simple in the eyes of the protagonists of that particular
position. While the issues I have in mind in this book are
important, they are peripheral to those central tenets of
Christianity that form the basis of judgements about
faithfulness or unfaithfulness. In addition, none of the
arguments are solely intellectual ones; they are also
social, political, moral, and spiritual — sometimes all
four, sometimes just one or two. But they are never
purely academic. Self-centred attitudes may readily
intervene, misunderstandings are frequently encountered, and therefore forgiveness is required. Whenever
controversy occurs, forgiveness is mandatory. Not only
this; forgiveness may prevent another controversy from
developing.

Once the intimate interrelationship of forgiveness and
controversy has been established, the importance of
forgiveness suggests that every effort should be made to
prevent, or at the least minimize, controversy. The radical ramifications of forgiveness as spelled out in this
chapter place an immense burden on Christians to deal
effectively and constructively with controversy. All who
claim to take forgiveness seriously have no choice but to
take controversy seriously as well.

The case may sound convincing but there is more to
be said, and to take the matter further we have to look at
what unity in the body of Christ might mean, and where
humility fits in.

Questions for group discussion

1. We frequently use the Pharisees as examples of how
    we should not behave and attitudes we should

avoid. Outline what you think were the major failings of the Pharisees.

2. List the similarities you see between the attitudes of many in our churches (including yourself?) and the Pharisees. Do you think it is dangerous to condemn the Pharisees as freely as we frequently do?

3. In this chapter, hypocrisy is recognized as the biggest stumbling block for Christians. Do you agree with this assessment? Compare the problems produced by hypocrisy with the problems produced by false doctrine.

4. Should we take account of the viewpoints (with which we disagree) of other Christians, to such an extent that we are prepared to modify our own viewpoints?

5. Think of a situation where you have had a disagreement with another Christian, and ask yourself to what extent forgiveness has entered the picture.

6. How would you react if the pastor or vicar of your church indulged in some social activity of which you disapproved? Perhaps he spends too much money on attending concerts, or is involved competitively in motor racing (think of anything that stirs you up) — where does criticism come into the picture?

FIVE

Living for Others

Unity in the body of Christ

This is crucial for Christians in relating to other Christians. Jesus himself stressed the importance of unity between his followers in his high priestly prayer (Jn. 17:20–23) and it was repeatedly referred to by the writers of the New Testament letters. Paul, for instance, in writing to the disciples at Ephesus, urged the people there to make every effort to maintain their unity and peace, since he regarded these as marks of the work of the Holy Spirit (Eph. 4:1–6).

Unity can best be understood by using the picture of a human body (Rom. 12:4–8; 1 Cor. 12:12–31; Eph. 4: 7–16). All parts of a body are essential for its normal functioning. We all know how incapacitated we feel once any part of our body begins to malfunction, whether this be a tooth (in the form of toothache), blood vessels in the head (in the form of a headache), or the gastrointestinal tract (in the form of indigestion). Such indisposition is minor compared to breaking a leg, and suddenly finding oneself confined to a wheelchair or dependent on crutches, let alone compared to major or terminal illness. No matter what the illness, whether short-term and minor or long-term and major, the point is the same — the integrity of our body has been threatened, and the unity of its functioning has been disturbed. The body no longer functions as it should, and our lives are changed for the worse.

In exactly the same way we all need each other within the body of Christ, both at a local and at worldwide levels. The power of the analogy stems from that which we are so aware of in our own bodies. Unfortunately, we are not nearly as aware of the effects of disruption to the body of Christ. Perhaps we are so used to seeing it function sub-optimally, that we are tragically unaware of its potential. If this is the case, the analogy becomes all the more important. Christians cannot function in isolated units: we cannot ignore the influence of other Christians (whether for good or for ill). We are inter-related, just as each individual cell in our liver or brain cannot function if other liver or brain cells around it are malfunctioning. Similarly, a well-functioning and faithful Christian cannot exist in a vacuum, but is pulled down when surrounded by Christians who are judgemental, schismatic, and vindictive.

The significance of unity within the body of Christ cannot be ignored. Of course, it's important to know how to interpret this picture, and I have no wish to underestimate its many ramifications. But the picture and its power have to be retained. Think of the gifts of the Spirit (1 Cor. 12:1–31; 14:1–39). Various gifts have been given by Christ to his church, to be used for strengthening the Christian community (Eph. 4:11–13). To keep them to ourselves, is to deny them to other Christians, and this leads to a weakening of the body of Christ. Similarly, Christ's body is weakened when we prevent one Christian from ministering to another, and much more so when we deny that another Christian is even a member of Christ's body.

The unity of the body of Christ implies that we are to be open to fellowship with all others who acknowledge the saving work of Christ on the cross and who demonstrate something of that work in the quality of their lives. These other Christians will undoubtedly include those with whom we have profound disagreements on a whole range of matters, other than those central to Christian belief and practice. Nevertheless, if we have a high view of the unity of the body of Christ, we can neither downgrade nor ostracize other Christians on the ground that we differ from them over political, ethical, or even certain theological questions. To shut out from our sphere of influence another Christian (or Christian group) with the potential of ministering to us, is like denying the existence of an essential part of our bodies, something that can lead to disastrous and bizarre results.

We have to demonstrate *categorically* that a person is not a Christian (and therefore by definition not a member of Christ's body), before denying the validity of that person's contribution to the body of Christ. Before even contemplating such a path, we should look very closely at the criteria for membership of Christ's body (as outlined at the beginning of chapter 3). This should never be considered without a great deal of self-assessment and prayer.

The body of Christ and controversy

The unity of Christ's body should constitute the prime impetus to resolution of conflict between Christians. As long as the essential integrity of the gospel concerning the person and work of Christ is maintained, nothing is of sufficient importance to cause schisms within the church. Everything else should be regarded as peripheral and open to honest debate. Some will disagree, and will argue that membership of churches in some denominations bestows legitimacy upon non-biblical views. Hence, the argument goes, it is crucial that evangelical Christians reject such associations, and that if they don't they themselves are schismatic. It's not my purpose to argue for or against specific views such as this, except to say that enormous care is required at this point. The denunciation of fellow-evangelical Christians on the grounds of their denominational allegiance separates one Christian from another, even though it has the opposite intention. There is no escape from this; the end result is yet further controversy on an issue that is not ultimately central to Christianity.

The centrality of Christ as Lord and Saviour is the emphasis that leads to unity of his body, the church. Without this emphasis, we always have a fall-back position, namely, that the Christian with whom we disagree is not of our calibre, or is associated with Christian elements of which we disapprove. As long as this holds, controversy can be freely entered into with apparent justification; controversy that may well end in a breaking of fellowship. On the other hand, when the unity of the body of Christ becomes our focus, it also becomes the driving-force in our dealings with other Christians.

We have to learn how to live with one another in love, and also how to disagree with one another in love. It necessitates entering into dialogue with one another while retaining respect for the integrity and spirituality of the other. It involves praying for those Christians with whom we disagree, speaking with them, reading their books, listening to their sermons, and sincerely seeking to learn from them. It involves being prepared to test all our views on social and spiritual matters against the general principles found in Scripture. Sometimes, we will be wrong and will have to admit that we were wrong. But even if convinced that we are correct, we may still have a great deal to learn from our adversaries, and we will recognize our constant need of one another within the body of Christ.

When serious regard is paid to unity in the body of Christ, unresolved controversy with other Christians becomes a matter of the utmost seriousness. It won't solve any disputes by itself, but it will prevent us from treating such disputes as though they were of minor consequence. It's a poignant reminder that to weaken Christ's body by separation from other members of his body, or simply by ignoring their contribution (or even existence), is precisely that — a weakening of the witness to Christ in a secular world. Whether or not separation from another Christian group is ever justified, is an extremely contentious matter; after all, the Reformation was a separation from the Roman Catholic Church, although the grounds for it were profound and serious. It is not for me to enter this debate, except to say that the many lesser separations that occur constantly today, should impress upon us the enormity of the problem that encompasses all Protestant Christians. Separation at a denominational level cannot be used to justify separation from one another at an individual level. It is to our shame that we have become so immune to the everyday tragedy of institutional separation that we fail to take sufficiently seriously the indivisibility of the body of Christ. A sceptical world expects more of us, and rightly so.

Controversy that divides churches and individual Christians is a totally unacceptable witness; even worse, it is a tragically negative witness. We neither honour nor glorify the Lord by this, and those in the world around us turn away in disgust and confusion.

Humility

Few themes are as dominant in the New Testament as that of humility (Lk. 14:7–14; Phil. 2:3, 4): we are not to think of ourselves more highly than we ought (Rom. 12:3, 4). In other words, all that we are, comes from God. Whatever we have in the way of abilities, gifts (both natural and spiritual), and position in society, comes from him. To think highly of ourselves is, therefore, a contradiction in terms for Christians, who are to realize their total dependence upon God's mercy. And so it is inappropriate to advance our own interests; we are to live for others, to acknowledge their interests and seek to advance those interests.

> Now I want you to know, brothers, that what has happened to me has really served to advance the gospel. As a result, it has become clear throughout the whole palace guard and to everyone else that I am in chains for Christ. Because of my chains, most of the brothers in the Lord have been encouraged to speak the word of God more courageously and fearlessly.
>
> It is true that some preach Christ out of envy and rivalry, but others out of good will. The latter do so in love, knowing that I am put here for the defence of the gospel. The former preach Christ out of selfish ambition, not sincerely, supposing that they can stir up trouble for me while I am in chains. But what does it matter? The important thing is that in every way, whether from false motives or true, Christ is preached. And because of this I rejoice.
>
> Yes and I will continue to rejoice.
>
> Philippians 1:12–18

Paul was in prison for the sake of the gospel and there existed a distinct possibility that he would be put to death. Conditions were harsh, and he was chained continually to Roman soldiers. As one would expect, Paul was far from glib about his situation, and yet, because of where he was and because of the way in which he coped with it, the gospel spread among the Roman guards, and other Christian prisoners were encouraged.

The unexpected feature here is that Paul's situation was made even worse by the actions of some people in the church — they were doing their best to make life difficult for him while, at the same time, they preached Christ. There was personal rivalry; their preaching was from mixed motives. Paul's immediate response was not one of self-protection. In spite of having reason to query their motives, he concluded that this didn't matter since they were making Christ known. In acknowledging the

positive rather than negative aspects of their preaching,
he recognized a major difference between these particular people and the many false teachers, who were dis-
torting the gospel and not preaching Christ. What did
matter to Paul was that the gospel of Christ was being
proclaimed, and because of this he could rejoice. This is
in direct contrast to a judgemental reaction which would
have condemned them, judged their motives, and possibly ended in a public quarrel.

> Whatever happens, conduct yourselves in a manner
> worthy of the gospel of Christ. Then, whether I come and
> see you or only hear about you in my absence, I will
> know that you stand firm in one spirit, contending as one
> man for the faith of the gospel without being frightened
> in any way by those who oppose you. This is a sign to
> them that they will be destroyed, but that you will be
> saved — and that by God. For it has been granted to you
> on behalf of Christ not only to believe on him, but also to
> suffer for him, since you are going through the same
> struggle you saw I had, and now hear that I still have.
> If you have any encouragement from being united
> with Christ, if any comfort from his love, if any fellow-
> ship with the Spirit, if any tenderness and compassion,
> then make my joy complete by being like-minded, hav-
> ing the same love, being one in spirit and purpose.
>   Philippians 1:27–30; 2:1, 2

As Paul works through his response to this situation,
he concludes that the task before him is to magnify
Christ by what he, Paul, is and does. He is to go on
living for others and serving them. But there is also a
common task — that of believing in Christ and suffering
for him. From this, certain things follow. We should
encourage and strengthen one another to demonstrate
our love for one another. This is because the Holy Spirit
creates a fellowship, not only between us as individual
believers and God, but also between us as believers
among each other. Since Christ has done the same work
in all our lives, and since we have all experienced the
love of Christ, we should be demonstrating this love

without reserve or discrimination in our response to others.

For Paul it is not sufficient to boast about oneness in Christ; we also have to *demonstrate* it in unequivocal terms. 'Make my joy complete', Paul writes, 'by being like-minded, having the same love.' We are to have the same thoughts and goals, thinking through issues together, and being agreed on the things that really matter. We are to share the love of Christ in a meaningful way together, learning what it means to act and to react as Christ himself would have done, and in everything ensuring that our actions clearly demonstrate our unity.

Unity among Christians is vital for authenticating the reality of the gospel, and therefore for enabling the gospel to spread. But it's not only a unity in what we believe (important as that is); it's a unity in how we function together as God's people. There's not much virtue in a church (or any Christian community), perfectly united on its doctrinal basis, if the people making up that church are unable to live with each other without backbiting, petty jealousies, and pointless rivalries. What those outside the Christian community see is the extent to which Christians love each other, the manner in which we cope with genuine differences of opinion and clashes of personality, and the degree to which we accept into our midst the outsiders, the non-conformists, and the disadvantaged. Those outside our boundaries are not particularly concerned about whether we are all pro-lifers, ecstatic tongue-speakers, premillenialists, convinced anti-paedobaptists, or capitalists. On the other hand, our attitudes towards each other, and our concern for those in need, are critical pointers to what we are really like: they are indicators of our faithfulness or otherwise as followers of Jesus Christ.

Putting the interests of others first

Do nothing out of selfish ambition or vain conceit, but in humility consider others better than yourselves. Each of

you should look not only to your own interests, but also
to the interests of others. Your attitude should be the
same as that of Christ Jesus:

Who, being in very nature God, did not consider
equality with God something to be grasped, but made
himself nothing, taking the very nature of a servant,
being made in human likeness. And being found in
appearance as a man, he humbled himself and became
obedient to death — even death on a cross! Therefore
God exalted him to the highest place and gave him the
name that is above every name, that at the name of Jesus
every knee should bow, in heaven and on earth and
under the earth, and every tongue confess that Jesus
Christ is Lord, to the glory of God the Father.

Philippians 2:3–11

But how do we put these attitudes into practice?
Paul's answer is that we put the interests of others
before our own interests, and that we consider the
legitimate needs of others rather than our own sometimes selfish desires. There's no place for rivalry and
personal vanity. On the contrary, we have to seek the
good of others, even when they themselves are selfish.
Such a standard appears hopelessly idealistic and exceedingly remote from the harsh realities of the everyday world, where promotion of self reigns supreme —
sometimes even in Christian circles. What Paul is advocating is only possible by humility on our part.

What do we mean by humility? For Paul it was
summed up in what he knew of Christ. Our attitude
should be the same as Christ's; although he was the
eternal God, he laid aside his glory and became one of
his creation. He emptied himself of all he had been from
the foundation of the world and, in becoming human,
he became a servant. Christ put the interests of others
before his own interests. What is so remarkable is, that
the 'others' were his creation, those whom he had
brought into existence, who were below him and who
had rebelled against him. This was the path of humility
and self-emptying.

But even more was to come since Christ was prepared to die for others and to die a death considered a curse by the Jews — death on a cross. Christ gave up everything, voluntarily, freely. Paul emphasized this as a reminder to his readers that they were to put the interests of others before their own interests. Extreme as this position may appear, it can't be compared to the actions of Christ, who gave pre-eminence to the interests, not of those who were equal to him, but of those who were inferior to him.

And so, when confronted by a conflict situation, we are to put the interests of our antagonists first. This doesn't mean we are to demean ourselves and belittle our arguments, as though everything we stand for is worthless and what our antagonists stand for, valuable. It's a matter of considering seriously the stance and attitudes of the other person, seeking to understand why they hold that particular position. It's an attempt to place ourselves in the shoes of our antagonist, so that we get a feel for this alternative perspective.

Any such stance is going to require hard work and will undoubtedly prove demanding. We may contend that life is too short to be this scrupulous, that it is demanding enough working out the details of our own position, let alone the position of someone with whom we disagree and whom we may consider seriously in the wrong. And yet, if an issue is sufficiently important for debate and controversy, it's sufficiently important to demand a thorough assessment of the major competing viewpoints. Simply stating our own point of view and failing to address the alternative positions, is to relinquish our responsibility of digging for the truth.

Living for one's opponents

Christians, therefore, are not at liberty to deal in an offhand or derisory manner with those whom they class as opponents. Two matters are at stake: our own humility, and truth. Once we accept the importance of humility, others and their perspectives have to be taken seriously, however much we may disapprove of them. The interests of those persons are to be placed above our own interests, so that we are to be more concerned with supporting and understanding them than with promulgating our own perspective. This doesn't mean we downgrade what we stand for, but it does mean that we seek to understand the other person. This is a small thing to do when compared with the actions of Christ, who became human in order to experience what we experience.

Put another way, we are no longer living for ourselves but for Christ (2 Cor. 5:15). This means we also live for his people, including those of his people with whom we disagree. If Jesus is Lord of our lives, he is also Lord of those Christians with whom we disagree. It is not for us to judge these people. If Jesus is Lord of someone with whom I disagree, it is arrogant of me to denounce that person. To do so is to reject someone whom Jesus accepts. It is the opposite of humility.

Even more generally, we are to love our neighbours as ourselves. This leads to servanthood, as demonstrated by Jesus who came to serve and not to lord it over his fellow-beings. His supremacy lay in the quality of his self-giving, in the extent to which he put the claims of others above the claims that were rightfully his. He lived, not for his own satisfaction, but in order to bring fulfilment and wholeness to others. Jesus' washing his disciples' feet is a metaphor of servanthood and humility that derives its power from Jesus' willingness to wash the feet of all who were present (Jn. 13:1–11). Humility demands washing the feet of one's opponents as well as those of one's friends. There is no room for selectivity.

This is what humility is all about, and it is to be clearly expressed in the arena of conflict and disagreement. As we find ourselves in opposition to others, our chief concern should not be to win an argument but to ensure that truth prevails and that the welfare of those opposing us is upheld. These were the points stressed by Paul as he instructed the Ephesian Christians to speak truthfully to their neighbours, to be kind and compassionate to one another, and to forgive one another, because God had forgiven them in Christ (Eph. 4:25, 32). Paul went on to warn against any talk that would destroy others; against talk, even, that failed to build them up (Eph. 4:29). Humility is not concerned, therefore, with the negative alone; it aims to strengthen and help those opposed to us. It considers their welfare, even when we disagree with what they are doing or saying.

This was spelled out in considerable detail by James, who warned against envy and selfish ambition and who diagnosed the cause of fights and quarrels as self-centred desire (Jas. 3:9–4:3). A poignant illustration of this is provided by Diotrephes, who sought leadership in the church at all costs (3 Jn. 9, 10). His ambition led to malicious gossip and lies, and an unwillingness to welcome and accept fellow-Christians. Unfortunately, he loved to be first, and inevitably this led him to ostracize other leaders in the church. The end result of such desires is always the institutionalization of unresolved conflict. Diotrephes was the antithesis of humility, and he demonstrated what can happen when humility is replaced by arrogance.

Quarrels and dissension

A major obstacle to moving in the direction of openness is the ease with which we erect rigid rules encompassing details of beliefs, attitudes and practices. Those who obey these rules are accepted; those who reject them or disobey them are judged and rejected. All too easily such rules lead to judgementalism; they form the basis on which judgements are made and detract from the freedom and responsibility found in Christ.

It is no wonder, then, that Paul instructed the Colossian Christians not to 'let anyone judge you by what you eat or drink, or with regard to a religious festival, a New Moon celebration or a Sabbath day' (Col. 2:16). His argument was that rules are generally based on human commands and teachings which will ultimately disappear. All too often they are arbitrary and reflect circumstances occurring at one time and in one place. They may appear to be wise, but in the final analysis they are invariably limiting and perhaps misleading; they may even be valueless (Col. 2:21–23). The tragedy is that rules enable people to judge one another. If I obey a particular rule and you don't, I must by definition have a higher standard than you. This is used to justify my looking down on you, and judging you as being of less value than me. Unfortunately, in exactly the same way, someone else with their own set of rules can condemn me for failing to keep one of their rules. It results in a bewildering maze of competing sets of rules. They demean all that Christ bestowed upon us because they replace his wisdom by human standards, with inevitable, built-in limitations and, sometimes, sinful overtones.

There are many examples in the New Testament, and particularly in the New Testament letters, of the way in which rules and regulations were misused and led to quarrelling and dissension. Jesus met this problem repeatedly in his dealings with the Pharisees. In one of those instances, he was asked why his disciples didn't abide by various ancient traditions, such as washing their hands before meals (Matt. 15:1–9). Instead of answering the question directly, Jesus rounded on the Pharisees by accusing them of breaking the tradition in much more important ways, by rationalizing central features of it: they found a way around having to honour their fathers and mothers. Although it appeared on the surface that they honoured their parents, they actually nullified God's law. By being hypocrites, they were able to ignore the central issues and concentrate instead on external minutiae, such as the importance of hand-washing. Their motives were wrong, as is often the case when rules and regulations are given a place of great significance.

Another illustration of this issue is provided by the incident when Jesus was challenged about his use of the Sabbath day (Jn. 7: 19–24). He was criticized for healing on the Sabbath day, rather than keeping the day in accordance with the law of Moses. But for Jesus to bestow wholeness upon a person was more in keeping with God's will. Jesus' rejoinder to the Pharisees consisted of a warning against making superficial judgements, which by definition are unjust. From this we can infer that it is vitally important that we never judge on the basis of inadequate criteria and, almost without exception, criteria based on rules and regulations are inadequate. It's essential to look behind the obvious and ask what principles are at stake. We need to ask why certain regulations (or beliefs) are important, and whether they are as important as we like to make out. We also need to ask whether they hinder some people, and whether they constitute a source of division between us (or our group) and other Christians.

Group factions

One of the formidable obstacles in working out these principles, is the existence of factions (Gal. 5:20), groups of people who narrow down what they have in common to one issue or one area of agreement. Their motive for this may be exemplary, and yet it easily becomes associated with a party-spirit, selfish ambition, dissension, and envy. Very readily, what becomes important is allegiance to the group, and outward impressions become crucial (Gal. 6:12). This leads almost inevitably to the elevation of secondary matters, which are readily converted into matters of primary concern. It occurred in the early church in relation to circumcision, and it happens today with many secondary issues. If, for instance, we are prepared to separate from fellow-Christians on questions of nuclear warfare, feminism, or abortion, we are implicitly claiming that nuclear warfare, feminism, and abortion, are all of greater importance than the work of Christ on the cross. We are making a peripheral issue, no matter how important in its own right, into a central one, and in doing this are displacing Christ from the centre of institutional Christianity.

The emergence of factions is not an isolated phenomenon, but is what Paul describes as behaviour belonging to the 'sinful [lower] nature' (Gal. 5:19). By this, he refers to behaviour such as jealousy, fits of rage, envy, selfish ambition, dissensions, and jealousy (Gal. 5:20, 21). Attitudes that lead to factionalism are the antithesis of humility, since humility has as its goal maintenance of the unity of the body of Christ. This applies regardless of which issues are leading to the emergence of factions. In spite of this, factions are frequently justified because of the particular doctrine(s) that appears to be at stake. However, no doctrine, regardless of its importance, justifies factionalism — in which squabbling, excessive ambition, and a desire for power dominate all else.

All thinking and discussion about the possibility of separating from other Christians should be carried out within an atmosphere of love, joy, peace, and kindness (Gal. 5:22–25). Separation may be the ultimate way forward, but it should always be accompanied by deep regret that Christ's body will be disrupted. Regret, however, is only made possible by an atmosphere of love and peace, with valiant attempts being made at personal reconciliation. Separation always signifies defeat, and is always a mark of our inability to understand and come to terms with a perspective different from our own. So often, though, it is not a clear-cut case of right and wrong, and we need the grace to admit this even when we cling resolutely to our own perspective. In this way, we avoid the tragedy of factionalism.

Unfortunately, there are many examples of quarrelling, sometimes resulting in divisions, within church leadership. It is amply borne out by the divisions Paul found in Corinth.

> Brothers, I could not address you as spiritual but as worldly — mere infants in Christ. I gave you milk, not solid food, for you were not yet ready for it. Indeed, you are still not ready. You are still worldly. For since there is jealousy and quarrelling among you, are you not worldly? Are you not acting like mere men? For when one says, 'I follow Paul,' and another, 'I follow Apollos,' are you not mere men?
>
> What, after all, is Apollos? And what is Paul? Only servants, through whom you came to believe — as the Lord has assigned to each his task. I planted the seed, Apollos watered it, but God made it grow. So neither he who plants nor he who waters is anything, but only God, who makes things grow. The man who plants and the man who waters have one purpose, and each will be rewarded according to his own labour. For we are God's fellow-workers; you are God's field, God's building.
>
> 1 Corinthians 3:1–9

For Paul, the jealousy and strife in this church illustrated lives lived on what he described as the human level, as opposed to the spiritual level. They were living for themselves and not for others, demonstrating self-centredness and arrogance.

There were factions within the church, some with allegiance to Apollos and others to Paul. One imagines that these factions were seen by their perpetrators as offering different strengths for the life of the church. Paul himself acknowledges this, in that he recognizes that whereas he commenced the work, Apollos was responsible for carrying it on; he sowed the seed and Apollos watered it. There's no problem in this, as long as it's recognized that God is behind every facet of the work; God made the seed grow. The trouble comes when the contribution of one is pitted against the con-

tribution of another; Paul *versus* Apollos. This is quite
different from Paul *and* Apollos, where the respective
contributions of the two are recognized and are seen as
complementing each other.

A confrontational model is the outcome of a fundamental misunderstanding, in that a work of God has
been reduced to a work of human beings. This is true
even when one of the human beings is as influential as
Paul. The tragedy is that the actions of God have been
glossed over and are acknowledged only as the actions
of humans. This is a tragedy of immense dimensions,
reflecting, as it does, a major misunderstanding of what
Christianity is; for Paul it demonstrated the spiritual
immaturity of this Corinthian church.

Factions, such as these, stem from a confrontational
situation. Paul completely rejected this, since he considered that both he and Apollos were performing the
tasks allotted to them by the Lord. The success of the
venture was not ultimately dependent on their efforts,
but on God. What was required of them was faithfulness
to God in carrying out their appointed tasks; they were
merely the gardeners (important as gardeners are). They
were to work as a team, not as rival combatants. For
Paul the analogy was not to be one of warfare, but of
fellow-workers; we might prefer the model of fellow-
players in the same team. One could equally well look
upon them as parts of the same body, functioning together as integral components of a larger whole.

Although I've dealt with this episode in terms of the
church, since this is the context of the Corinthian passage, it applies outside specific churches. In the wider
Christian community (including para-church organizations) cliques develop, sometimes centred around a personality and sometimes around an issue. Cliques may
then produce their own organizations, Bible colleges,
and magazines. It doesn't take much for one clique to
emerge as the rival of another one, condemning much
that the other clique stands for.

The emergence of rival cliques is sometimes under-

standable, and there may be situations where it is difficult to see how the tide of factionalism can be stemmed.
When faced by such a predicament, one has to ask what
occurred prior to the factionalism. Was it leading almost
inexorably towards that tragic end? While such an end
was undoubtedly never intended, an ever-increasing
narrowness of outlook and its associated judgementalism can only terminate at this point, by which time it
is too late to avert it.

The dangers of speculation

Up to now I have made a distinction between central
Christian beliefs and peripheral ones (chapter 3). In
doing this, I've had in mind those beliefs that are crucial
to what it means to be a Christian according to the
teaching of the Bible, and those beliefs which, while
important, are not crucial to the gospel. As we have
seen, peripheral beliefs include views on issues such as
baptism, prophecy, the nature of the church, the gifts of
the Spirit, warfare (including nuclear warfare), the role
of women in the church, the method of creation, the
precise value placed on human and animal life, and
environmental concerns. There are differences of opinion on all these matters; they have to be taken seriously
and argued through constructively. Although these are
significant issues and should be treated as such, great
care should be taken to prevent them usurping too
central a role in Christianity.

When we move into the realm of 'speculation', we
move into a grey area where secondary matters are
regarded as primary ones. The early church had problems in this area, with teachers who urged them to pay
undue attention to minor matters, generally of a Jewish
nature. These included what Paul referred to as myths
and genealogies (1 Tim. 1:4), verbal questions and quib-
bles (1 Tim. 6:4, 5), foolish and ignorant speculations
(2 Tim. 2:23, 24), foolish speculations, genealogies, quar-

rels, and controversies over the law (Tit. 3:9), and mere human injunctions (Col. 2:20–23). They included prescriptions that took away the freedom these new Christians had in Christ and have much in common with what I have previously called rules and regulations.

What they did was to force Christians to behave according to certain stipulations, generally about what they were to eat, drink, taste, touch, and the festivals they were to observe. For us the details are unimportant. What is important is that these minor matters were highly speculative, even if they had originated from something of substance. A belief or stipulation had been taken out of context, probably magnified and modified far beyond the original intention, and this was then foisted on Christians as though it was of central importance. If they failed to take account of it, they were accused of nullifying something of major significance. Consequently, something of no substance and probably of dubious validity became of greater importance than the death of Christ on the cross. With it went a loss of their new-found freedom in Christ, to be replaced by a bondage just as bad as any bondage they had previously experienced as non-Christians.

We, in Western societies, are not confronted with the same type of dubious speculations; our major temptation is to so concentrate on a minor issue that we convert it into a principle of central importance. But viewpoints on minor issues are by their very nature speculative, or at least subject to varying interpretations. The unfortunate consequence of this is that a speculative idea is put forward as though it had far more authority within a theological tradition than it actually has. There are well-known situations where membership of certain churches, para-church groups, or Christian schools has depended on acceptance of a premillenialist perspective, a particular (pro- or anti-) position on the charismata, a creationist stance, or a pro-life viewpoint. In each of these cases, the positions being advocated are not unequivocally biblical. Each of a range of viewpoints may have valid biblical backing. There are also speculative elements in adopting specific applications for church life or society today; some applications may be far removed from the biblical principles on which they are thought to be based. In other cases they may be invested with a strong cultural element.

When confronted by an insistence that particular stances on such issues are crucial to the Christian faith, we begin to see that they have a great deal in common with the speculations confronting the early church. What is the difference between stressing the all-importance of certain festivals or of what we eat and drink, and the all-importance of the timing of certain events accompanying the second coming of Christ or of the precise method by which God brought the physical universe into existence? We cannot be certain about the details of these events and if we dwell excessively upon the speculative details, we quickly overlook the theological truths they convey. Whenever this occurs, we have fallen into the speculative trap.

I am greatly dismayed when I read books that tell me in vast detail and with immense certainty the events that occurred at the beginning of time, but which gloss over the character and purposes of God. It is hard to believe that Genesis was written as a science textbook for twentieth century Western people, but has little to say to people of all cultures and at all periods of history about the manner in which God upholds everything by his power, and about the value God has bestowed upon his creation. In this instance, speculative 'science' has replaced a God-centred theology, even though this may not be the intention of those who hold a scientific creationist position. My concern is not with the latter *per se*, but with any system that allows this displacement to occur. When the lordship of Christ appears to have become subsidiary to a speculative scheme of creation, our emphases have become dangerously skewed.

Speculations of this type are unprofitable and pointless, and lead to controversy and strife (Tit. 3:9). They breed quarrels, whereas the servant of the Lord is not to be quarrelsome (2 Tim. 2:24). In short, this sort of activity leads nowhere, and breeds dissension and unrest since the issues remain unresolved. There are different sides to the arguments, and different legitimate perspectives on both sides. It is hardly surprising then, that when one position is put forward as *the* true expression of Christianity, others will rebel. Not only is confrontation inevitable, but it occurs over subsidiary matters. The gospel itself is not at stake, but the quarrelling that ensues detracts *from* the gospel and directs people's attention away from the glory and majesty of God and his purposes.

Judgement and rebuke

In James 4:11, 12, James warns his readers against disparaging one another. His reasoning is that whoever passes judgement on another Christian, disparages the Law and judges it. In other words, to judge the Law is to sit in judgement on it, and this is akin to acting as God. Since this is folly, James concludes that we are in no position to judge our neighbour.

On the other hand, there is another emphasis in Paul's writings, and this is that Christians *are* to judge those inside the church.

> What business is it of mine to judge those outside the church? Are you not to judge those inside? God will judge those outside. "Expel the wicked man from among you."
>
> 1 Corinthians 5:12, 13

Although Christians are to refrain from judging those outside the church, a different principle seemingly applies to those inside the church. This applies, in particular, to those who are immoral or idolatrous, slanderers, drunkards, or swindlers. As with the Pharisees, the stress is on the quality of life of these people, and not on their beliefs.

At first glance this is at odds with the non-judgemental ethos I've been advocating. Surely, to root out the evildoer is to judge the evildoer; it's certainly not turning a blind eye to their indiscretions. This is true, but not at variance with the role I've already assigned to discernment. The people being criticized in Corinth were deliberate and flagrant in their misdemeanours. They appeared to flout their wrongdoing, but at the same time claimed to belong to a Christian fellowship. It wasn't a case of discovering that someone had slipped up at one point, had fallen into sin on some matter, or had great difficulty in overcoming a constant temptation in their lives.

Those in Corinth were persistent and overt offenders. They made a mockery of all that the gospel stands for. They weren't just sinners saved by God's grace who had fallen from that grace, but were those whose lifestyles were blatantly at variance with the standards of the Christian gospel. This wasn't a case of bigoted, self-righteous people trying to trip up a fellow-Christian, but of the whole community being scandalized by a lifestyle that made a mockery of Christ's attitudes and of his self-sacrificial death on the cross. These people were self-centred and crudely hedonistic; they were a blight on any Christian community.

In one respect these people were judging themselves, and the Christians were simply making plain what was evident to everyone around them. There *is* a role for judgement like this, but it is the only circumstance in which judgement is allowed to take place. This is not to be used as a rationale for throwing Christians out of a Christian community because they are not prepared to conform to every aspect of lifestyle or beliefs laid down by that community. That is an illustration of manufacturing strictures not found in the gospel, and it very

rapidly leads to the sort of pharisaic judgementalism
that is contrary to the thrust of the gospel.

Further light on the matter of rebuke is found in the
contrast between Jesus' relationship with his disciples
on the one hand, and with Judas on the other. Jesus was
explicit in his rebuke of the disciples, but with Judas he
generally avoided confrontation until the last moment
(the week before he was betrayed).

In talking to his disciples, Jesus sometimes rebuked
them mildly (Mk. 4:40; 7:17–19) and sometimes severely
(Matt. 16:23). He pointed out their lack of perception
(Mk. 8:14–21), slothfulness (Matt.17:17), pride (Lk.
9:46–48), lack of love (Lk. 9:51–56), self-righteousness
(Mk. 14:1–10), and lack of commitment (Mk. 14:37–41).
However, in his relationship with Judas, Jesus hinted
that Judas would betray him (Jn. 6:70, 71; 13:10, 11), but
only later in his ministry did he specifically state that it
was Judas who was the betrayer (Matt. 26:20–25; 26:45,
46; Lk. 22:48). The point at which Jesus confronted Judas
was the point at which Judas determined to go his own
way (Mk. 14:1–10; Jn. 13:10–21; 26–30).

This contrast illustrates the proverb that we are not to
rebuke a mocker, only a wise man (Prov. 9:7–9). There is
a tension here, since rebuking may either make the
situation worse or lead to healing. There may come a
point where confrontation is required, but it has to be
approached with a great deal of sensitivity. If there is
clear wrong, something has to be done about it, and yet
this is only to be done very gently, with the good of the
erring person at heart, and in the realization that we,
too, may be tempted (Gal. 6:1, 2). We are to carry the
loads of our fellow-believers, to help and encourage
them, and to assist them in every way possible.

Not only this, we should welcome the rebuke of
righteous people (Ps. 141:5). It's a means of growth in
understanding, since it broadens our horizons and pro-
vides us with additional hints and pointers at how best
to live as Jesus' followers. For some of us this is not easy,
and yet it is the path to maturity as Christians.

The Holy Spirit and controversy

> Dear friends, do not believe every spirit, but test the
> spirits to see whether they are from God, because many
> false prophets have gone out into the world. This is how
> you can recognise the Spirit of God: every spirit that
> acknowledges that Jesus Christ has come in the flesh is
> from God, but every spirit that does not acknowledge
> Jesus is not from God. This is the spirit of the antichrist,
> which you have heard is coming and even now is
> already in the world.
>
> You, dear children, are from God and have overcome
> them, because the one who is in you is greater than the
> one who is in the world.
>
> 1 John 4:1–4

Since Christians have the Holy Spirit within them
(1 Jn. 4:1–4), it is not just *we* who know what the Spirit
wants, but all those who are children of God. It is what
distinguishes Christians from false teachers, and it is
what enables Christians to acknowledge that Jesus in
human form was indeed the Christ, that he was from
God, and that he was God in human form. All who
acknowledge this have the Holy Spirit directing them.

As we follow this through, we have to accept the
validity of the commitment of those with whom we may
disagree on many issues aside from these central ones.
We have to accept that other churches, traditions, and
communions owe their existence and allegiance to the
work of the Spirit, even though we may have serious
concerns about some of their emphases. We have to
accept that Christians who differ from us on many
issues, trust in the directing and leading of the Spirit. We
also need to acknowledge the power of the Holy Spirit
in their lives, including those occasions when their
stance is quite different from ours.

This is difficult for us because it breaks down the neat
barriers and divisions we erect. The result of these
divisions is that we find ourselves at a loss when
confronted by conflicting lifestyles, forms of worship, or

belief systems. We long to be assured that one of a
conflicting pair of possibilities is right, and the other is
wrong. But what if we cannot be sure? What if there is
truth in both, or at least partial truth in both? What do
we do then? Does this make rational Christian belief
impossible, or has everything become relative?

These are genuine difficulties and it is right that we
take them seriously. However, these difficulties do not
lead to intolerable relativism, neither should we throw
up our hands in despair. This apparent lack of certainty
is implicit within the Holy Spirit's leading, and is an
acknowledgement that we do not know everything on a
host of issues, many of which are complex. If we limit
our horizons, thinking that only those in our small circle
are correct and everyone else is wrong, we immediately
condemn the stand and motives of many others within
evangelicalism, let alone many outside it. It is perilously
close to those who see room in heaven for only 144,000,
when even those with the same views as themselves
number millions. There is something amiss with this
way of thinking, and we should beware lest we indulge
in it.

It is far more honest to acknowledge the existence
outside our group of many who have views of which we
may disapprove, and yet whose Christian credentials
cannot be faulted. Once this is faced openly, we should
ask the Holy Spirit for wisdom to accept truths we
cannot readily face and for openness to truths of which
we know little. We are to learn from others, even when
we wouldn't rush to participate in their activities or
accept all their beliefs. As long as we are unwilling to
learn from others, we are implicitly viewing them in a
judgemental spirit. Only as we are open to correction
ourselves and to a broadening of our vision, do we
begin to see what the church *is*, and do we begin to learn
more of the breadth of Christianity. We ourselves may be
wrong, and we need the Holy Spirit to be our guide and
teacher — sometimes using the experiences of fellow-
Christians.

This stance leads to a number of principles, all of which are relevant in dealing with controversy. The first is that we maintain a sense of proportion. When difficulties arise, they are to be approached with care and shouldn't be allowed to separate one Christian from another within the church. Second, it is important to be outward-looking, and not inward-looking. In this way, we gain a sense of proportion as we make ourselves aware of the contributions being made by other Christians. Without this, the temptation is to exclude the approach of others and to fail to recognize it as part of the kingdom of God. Third, we need to be flexible and accept that change is an integral part of the growth of the kingdom of God. This demands a willingness to adapt to new circumstances and new approaches; old ways are not automatically wrong or irrelevant, but a longing to follow the leading of the Holy Spirit in contemporary circumstances is necessary. Fourth, we need to focus our attention on God's provision for us as well as for other Christians. God will provide, no matter how dramatically circumstances change or how difficult it may be to come to terms with some of the changes, both within and outside the Christian community.

Salt and light

On the positive side, we are to be salt and light within society (Matt. 5:13–16). This well-known picture is of the church bringing flavour to the life of society, preserving it, and purifying it. Also within this picture is the possibility of the church failing to act in this way, losing its saltiness and failing to radiate light. But how do we function as salt and light?

We live in a judgemental society, and if we are judgemental towards one another, there is no difference between us and those around us. We live in a society characterized, all too often, by its aggressiveness, violence, spite, and anger. If we are like this, we will be indistinguishable from many around us. To be like others in these ways is to be part and parcel of the worldly spirit, leaving us no room to function as those who can purify and uplift society. In order to accomplish this, we have to be different, not in superficial, idiosyncratic ways, but by being genuinely forgiving, loving, and tender-hearted, just like Christ (Eph. 4:29–5:2).

We are, then, to love one another (1 Jn. 4:7–12), to live in harmony with one another (1 Pet. 3:8). We are never to prejudge someone who appears to have committed an obvious sin (1 Tim. 5:19–21); we are to act with strict impartiality. Timothy was instructed by Paul to turn a deaf ear to empty and worldly chatter (1 Tim. 6:20), because this is nothing more than a means of distracting us from important principles. Overall, therefore, we are to live at peace with one another. There is indeed a place for admonishing the careless, but this is always to be balanced by encouragement for the faint-hearted, and support for the weak, treating everyone with patience (1 Thess. 5:13, 14).

These are pointers to ways in which the church may act as salt and light within society. Without such characteristics, we have no reason to expect others to take us seriously. After all, if we constantly fail abysmally at these points, we have nothing others can admire: we are of no greater value than salt that has lost its saltiness. We fail the crucial test. The way in which we live together, coping with each other's foibles and limitations, is a mark of our likeness (or otherwise) to Christ.

Another means of approaching this topic is via one of Jesus' parables, the story of the Good Samaritan (Lk. 10:25–37). A lawyer, who wanted to vindicate himself, asked Jesus: 'Who is my neighbour?'. To this seemly, innocuous question, Jesus gave one of his totally unexpected replies, according to which religious people are not acting in neighbourly ways if they are unprepared to go to the aid of someone in distress. To act as a neighbour frequently involves sacrifice and cost; it may also involve getting one's hands dirty, and it may be danger-

ous. As in the story, it may involve crossing religious
and cultural boundaries, and perhaps criticism will be
incurred. In the picture painted by Jesus, being neighbourly shattered conventions, and would certainly have
led to the wrath and indignation of other religious
leaders.

To have given assistance to the man in trouble would
have created dissension among some of the religious
leaders. There would have been criticism of such an
action. On the other hand, to refuse to give assistance
was the antithesis of loving one's neighbour as oneself.
This is so often the case when Christians act as salt and
light. In showing leadership within society, they simultaneously create conflict among those close to them. The
shattering of commonly accepted conventions is itself
regarded as anathema.

Christians are not, therefore, to do everything possible
to avoid controversy. The prophetic ethos they should
enshrine will frequently lead to controversy. But we are
never to welcome controversy, and are never to stir it up
over minor issues. The type of controversy that may be
stirred up by acting as the good Samaritan results from
bringing Christians back to fundamentals, in this case
back to the quality of love to be demonstrated towards
others. This is a return to the values enshrined in the life
and attitudes of Christ; it is living Christianity.

Acting as salt and light highlights another contrast,
that between judgementalism and accountability. We are
accountable to each other, just as we are all accountable
to God. When this is the basis for our actions, we
recognize the importance of helping and encouraging
others, and being a model for them. For Christians,
judgement is to be replaced by accountability, since it is
in accountability, rather than in judgement, that we
learn to discern and demonstrate the mind of Christ.

As I make myself accountable to another, I open
myself to that other person. I am willing to learn from
them, as much as they may learn from me. I am prepared to be critically assessed by them, as together we

strive to live more in accordance with the will of God. Accountability and openness go hand in hand with openness to one another and, supremely, openness to the Spirit of the living Christ.

Questions for group discussion

1.   Discuss whether you find the picture of the body of Christ a helpful one when thinking about the church and how it functions.

2.   What type of church appeals to you? Is it one with a diverse range of people with different personalities, abilities, interests, backgrounds, and gifts, or is it one that is relatively homogeneous with people with whom you can readily identify because they are similar to you? Discuss the merits of these two extremes, and the church make-up you think is best able to function as the body of Christ.

3.   Humility, putting the interests of others first, and living for one's opponents, have been stressed in this chapter. Discuss whether you think it is possible to live in these ways in a highly competitive society. Are they a hindrance to getting on in business and the professions?

4.   Talk around the issue of group factions. Take Paul and Apollos as examples. Also think of some modern examples.

5.   Picture yourself as a church leader. How would you deal with a person in your church who is known to be devious in his business dealings?

6.   You have problems with Pentecostal churches, but a close colleague at work is a Christian and a Pentecostal. She embarrasses you when she speaks openly

in the canteen about the healings in her church. How do you react? What do you say to others? [For Pentecostals, put yourself in the position of having to cope with a Christian colleague who is never prepared to speak up as a Christian.]

SIX

Learning to Live with Controversy

Asking dangerous questions

Evangelicals are having difficulty in coming to terms
with differences on many social questions, because certain viewpoints are regarded by some as the only acceptable expressions of evangelical thought and action.
These stances have, therefore, been incorporated by
them (implicitly, if not explicitly) within the core of
doctrines considered essential to evangelicalism. These
may include conservative views on many economic,
defence, and evolutionary matters, as well as the ones of
particular concern to me personally, namely, bioethical
questions. To deviate from them is, in the eyes of some,
to court spiritual and moral disaster.

For people such as these a person can only be considered an evangelical if she or he believes in a free
market economy, is an advocate of nuclear deterrents, is
opposed to most forms of biomedical technology and/
or is a scientific creationist, and is a strident anti-
abortionist. The question is whether these issues should
be made *theological* watersheds?

But these areas are ones where there is a great deal of

uncertainty and unease within evangelicalism. If they assume theological significance, evangelicals will have allowed their uncertainty on these matters and their lack of theological expertise in them to control their thinking. What is required is serious theological reflection and widespread debate within evangelicalism, not short-term criticism of individual items of concern or the perceived shortcomings of other evangelicals.

Jesus didn't allow people to be divided over the washing of hands (Matt. 15:1–9; Lk. 11:37–44), or particular matters of the Law. He actually seemed to disdain such matters, and to play fast and loose over obedience of the Sabbath and even over adultery (Matt. 12:1–14; Jn. 8:1–11). This was because he always looked beyond any superficial interpretation to the underlying motives of those with whom he was dealing. In fact, he appeared to pay remarkably little attention to the divisions so regularly drawn by the Jewish authorities and by the leaders of Jewish opinion. He could hardly be described as a legalist (see chapter 4).

I'm not advocating a lack of all distinctions, but I am advocating a careful assessment of priorities. To place major emphasis on issues where there is considerable division of opinion and even uncertainty, is to turn upside down both Jesus' approach, and the approach normally adopted in other areas of our lives. It's to court immense danger, and the inevitable end result is a multitude of divisions, because the elevation of uncertainty to the status of decider of truth is fraught with ambiguity and catastrophic consequences. It's the way of sects and minority groups, with their constant search for an ever-narrower definition of the truth.

For people like myself, who are immersed in the debates of modern society, this path towards ever-increasing narrowness of vision can only lead to heresy hunts. In order to apply Christianity to modern questions, we need a vision that will enable us to recognize how Christian principles can be applied to questions and issues far removed from those found in Scripture.

This is a serious and demanding task, since we must grapple with injustice, inequality, and self-seeking where we find them within contemporary society. We must be engaged in the constant task of unpacking crucial biblical truths, and creatively seeking to apply these to the ordinary world around us. In doing this, we have to interpret what Scripture has to teach us.

Inevitably, some of our applications will be wrong, and on some occasions we will mislead others. Sometimes our interpretation of Scripture will be wayward. However, if we are faithful to our calling as Christians, seeking God's direction for our thinking as well as our living, the adventure can only be applauded. What this does mean is that we are moving far away from the safe attitudes that expect us to say and believe only what others are saying and believing. This is unacceptable in some quarters.

It raises a broader question, namely, whether there is a legitimate place within evangelicalism for those who are professionally trained in areas other than theology, and capable of exploring honestly and openly these other realms — whether science, medicine, economics, philosophy, politics, or the arts. The dilemma this poses is that those of us with such training bring to our Christian responses aspects of these other perspectives. There may well be a danger here, and this should not be under-emphasized. It's the danger of allowing these other perspectives to displace Christian perspectives and foundations. The remedy, however, is not to ignore these other perspectives, but to interpret them from a firm basis in Christian thinking.

What is needed is interdisciplinary exploration. Without this, the responses of evangelicals will owe far more to conservative attitudes (including conservative *theological* attitudes) than to serious, biblically-informed assessment (chapter 3). Evangelicals should be sketching out the common ground that exists between those in different disciplines: on this basis, serious dialogue becomes possible.

Making room for debate

Issues of public concern have long posed difficulties for the church. After many years of neglect evangelicals have now realized the importance of a Christian voice in political and social matters. This is good and it signifies a return to our ministry as salt and light within society (Matt. 5:13–16). Nevertheless, social involvement has its dangers and the one evident at present is the drive for a 'unified evangelical voice' on a range of issues within society, including biomedical ones such as abortion, homosexuality, and the status of the embryo and foetus, as well as various economic and political ones.

But why should all evangelicals be expected to advocate the same position on such issues? What is the virtue of all evangelicals saying that shops should be closed on Sundays, that all human embryos require precisely the same protection as you and me, that a particular conservative (or even liberal) political party is the only one to vote for, or that one's country should go to war over some particular cause? If all evangelicals spoke like this, they would be united for (or against) certain causes, but to what effect? In what way would that be relevant to the cause of the gospel? Would it even have an effect upon the societies in which we live?

We might ask whether there is any difference between advocating views such as these and deciding that all evangelicals should wear a certain type of clothing, or have their hair cut in a certain fashion. Were we to accept such proposals we would demonstrate our unity, but to what effect?

There are many issues that are of enormous seriousness, such as the spiritual meaning of communion or the need to curb the tragically high death rates among children in many developing countries of the world, on which we accept differences within Christian circles and feel no need to mount campaigns for a single Christian voice. Sometimes we are selective; and it has nothing to

do with the spiritual or moral value of the cause. It has
a great deal to do with social and political forces. If this
is the case, it behoves us to look very carefully at the use
of such causes to unite (and simultaneously divide)
Christians.

Concerns which are publicly popular are generally
not specifically evangelical or even Christian ones. They
may be in line with Christian interests, and it may be
valuable to have them brought to the forefront of public
debate. But this should be the thrust of campaigns,
allowing fellow-Christians who are not convinced by the
arguments to remain aloof. Diversity of opinions and
responses, and some open-endedness, must always be
allowed.

Any approach that explicitly denies the validity of this
type of diversity has adopted a pressure group mentality, according to which there is only one stance on an
issue acceptable within evangelicalism. Any deviation
from this rigid position is, by definition, a betrayal of the
evangelical cause. The result is that evangelicals are not
allowed to discuss in the public arena controversial
topics that have public implications.

Once the distinction between public polemic and private debate has been lost, practically all forums for
debate have been removed. Public speaking, writing,
and publishing are all, to some extent, public activities.
The desire for a unified evangelical voice implies that
what is spoken, written and published, must express
only one viewpoint — the authorized one. The implications of any such thrust are enormous. Not only is it
impossible to have serious debate within evangelical
circles on any contentious issues (that is bad enough),
but how does evangelicalism actually decide which
positions are, and which are not, acceptable?

If we are not very careful, there will be no forum for
open debate. An 'orthodox' position will not then be
arrived at by informed debate, but under the influence
of someone with a charismatic personality. From a position of power, such a person can ensure that all deviant

voices are silenced: by preventing those with alternative viewpoints from speaking at meetings, from being elected to positions of responsibility within Christian organizations, from publishing their views, or even from joining churches. This process is accelerated when the character and Christian standing of those holding opposing perspectives are berated. To be branded as liberal or heretic, or as likely to lead sincere Christians astray, constitutes good grounds for excluding them from Christian circles and for ensuring that their books or articles are not published by Christian publishing houses or Christian magazines. Even a private debate with them may be depicted as dangerous.

Such responses are understandable. The great difficulty is that these responses may be entirely secular in motivation, even though they are given a Christian gloss, and even though they may be held with great sincerity. It is frequently said by conservatives that some of the most dangerous people within the church are those who are warm, friendly and loving, but whose beliefs are destructive to the authority of the Bible. This may be so, but by the same token, those who exclude from the Christian community people with whom they disagree on minor issues, may be equally dangerous.

To give ourselves an authority that does not reside in us, is to give ourselves a status that is not ours to take. It is to confer upon ourselves the office of elder, bishop, or pastor, rather than looking to others within the Christian community to recognize whether God has indeed given us the gifts that fit us for such offices (1 Tim. 3:1–13). Such people are failing to recognize the significance of their place within the body of Christ. By making minor issues central, and by making themselves authoritative spokespeople on these issues, they are denigrating the whole concept of Christ's body. It is hardly surprising that so many Christian movements appear so secular.

Debate is essential on all issues affecting the vitality and witness of the church. Once debate is vanquished, someone has assumed a suspect leadership role. This does not mean that all viewpoints or beliefs are of equal value. It isn't the case, since our authority as evangelicals is the Bible, an authority that encourages rather than discourages serious thinking and intense debate.

Circumscribing debate on complex issues is akin to denying that complex issues exist. But they do exist. Unfortunately, complex issues are all too readily seen in simple terms with simple remedies. Apart from ignoring the reality of the human condition, the danger of this trend is that Christianity and the Christian gospel become transformed into little more than simple solutions for complex human problems. Very readily, the grandeur and majesty of Christian theology disappear, the gospel becomes unrecognizable, and the complex arguments of the apostle Paul are dismissed as hindrances to understanding simple Christianity.

Pressure groups

Evangelicals need to beware of forming pressure groups to advocate the rights and wrongs of single causes. Even should they succeed in wielding some political power in this way, it will be at the expense of oversimplifying issues and of becoming identified with a particular cause as much as with Christ. Pressure groups lend themselves to becoming schismatic, dividing the body of Christ for the sake of individual causes. But is any cause (however worthy in itself) of such importance that it is justifiable to destroy the unity of the body of Christ in an attempt to forward it? For me, the answer is 'no'.

Someone may argue, though, that some causes are far more important than others. It may be that pressure groups can be justified when important causes are at stake, but not over relatively unimportant ones. Let us imagine the following scenarios.

A church in a downtown neighbourhood — we'll call it church A — wants to keep the streets around it as wholesome as it can. As a result, when planning permission is sought to build an off-licence next door, it musters every argument it can to attempt to block this development. It argues that off-licences encourage the widespread availability of alcohol, and alcohol is one of the most pernicious influences within our society — breaking up family life, contributing to deaths on the road, and costing the community enormous sums of money in caring for those ravaged by its excessive use. However, having argued against the development using all the legitimate channels open to it, the people associated with the church cease their opposition when their case is not upheld. Not only this, but when the off-licence is built, they help those running it in many little ways, and even befriend the manager and his wife.

Now let's consider another church that finds itself in an identical situation. We'll call this church B. Confronted by an almost identical development, the church members decide that it's not sufficient simply to put forward a case against the off-licence. They have to stand up for the faith, and they have to be seen to be standing up for it. And so, once they realize that they have lost the planning battle, they form a physical barricade to attempt to stop workmen coming onto the site. They form themselves into a pressure group, and attempt to enlist the help of all who will support them, both Christian and non-Christian. They even feel that confrontation should be welcomed, because that will give them an opportunity to gain publicity for their cause. When confrontation ensues, they sing Christian songs as further witness; they are the Lord's people fighting his battle against the forces of evil, on this occasion in the guise of alcohol and lack of self-control. Some of them are arrested for their stand, some go to prison when they refuse to agree to be bound over to keep the peace. The church members are determined to fight this evil, and to gain recognition for their stand. They start an organization with headquarters in the church building and publish pamphlets in which they condemn not only those who drink alcohol (including Christians) but also those (again including Christians) who are prepared to argue that drinking alcohol is

not the greatest social and spiritual evil of the present
day.

Here we have two sets of Christians, faced with
identical situations, who respond to their situations
quite differently. Not only this, the views of both sets of
Christians on the matter confronting them — alcohol —
are the same. In other words, there is no theological
difference between them. Where they differ is in their
response to the situation and their handling of it. Those
in church A put forward their case as well as they can,
since they see this as their responsibility as Christians.
Having done this, they stop and then treat those next
door to them as their neighbours. Those in church B
consider that their faithfulness demands more, and that
they have to continue to stand against those disagreeing
with them on this particular matter.

Is alcohol a sufficiently important issue to go to the
lengths of those in church B? Some Christians will say
'yes' and agree with church B; others will say 'no' and
would adopt the same stance as those in church A; yet
others, will also say 'no', but would not even go as far as
those in church A. There are different perspectives on
this issue, even within the Christian community. Those
who advocate pressure group tactics on this particular
matter are not, therefore, speaking for all Christians, and
if they were to make this a matter of cardinal importance
for Christians they would simply succeed in separating
Christians from each other. A consequence of their actions and attitudes would be to elevate a particular
issue, in this instance alcohol, above all else within
Christianity.

This may be an unrepresentative example. I deliberately took as an illustration something we don't meet
routinely. But the way in which we respond to alcohol is
not the point as far as the principle of pressure groups is
concerned. Are we ever prepared to split the body of
Christ and separate ourselves from others for a cause

like this, one that is not central to the tenets of the Christian faith?

By their very nature, pressure groups are generally incompatible with the attitudes of Christ, since their only goal is to win the battle they are fighting, and defeat the opposition. Are any causes sufficiently serious to warrant this risk? How about the value of human life (whether abortion, or the persecution of minority groups), what about opposition to a notorious dictatorship that completely ignores human rights and dignity, or what about fighting government policies that seem dedicated to oppressing the weakest and most vulnerable within society? There is no difficulty in finding examples of injustice and oppression which any right-minded person, let alone any Christian, would oppose.

The issue at stake is not opposition to such policies. I take it that Christians should vigorously argue against them, and sacrificially do whatever they can to bring in a better way. What we are discussing is the setting up of pressure groups, with the aim to do whatever they can to bring certain selected practices to an end, opposing them and all who would in any way tolerate them. Perhaps it appears churlish even to question the legitimacy of pressure groups on some issues, and yet when they become the centre of attention and effort, no room is left for disagreement of any sort. They become all-exclusive, even excluding other Christians. Is any issue *that* significant, especially when Christ didn't appear to approach matters in such a way?

All too often pressure groups appear to want to bludgeon people into submission, including Christians. Not only this, but they tend to be selective and narrow in their spheres of interest and concern. If enormous care is not exercised they readily lack the all-encompassing compassion and concern so characteristic of Jesus. This is to be our way — not smug complacency and an easy life that ignores the injustices of society, but an approach that cares whenever human life and dignity are at stake.

In discussing pressure groups, my concern has been with pressure groups that identify a specific position on some issue as *the* Christian position. Many pressure groups, of course, have no such identification with Christianity, although Christians as individuals may support them (there are others Christians may vigorously repudiate). One can readily think of organizations advocating action on environmental matters, inadequate housing or support for the elderly, and abortion (both pro-life and pro-choice). The general arguments I've put forward apply with equal force to all pressure groups, although the dangers are greatest with specifically Christian ones. As such, I have more sympathy with Christians *as individuals* supporting secular pressure groups, as long as they do not expect all other Christians to do the same.

The dangers of dogmatism

Dogmatism is the opposite of humility, since it allows no room for error. And yet, as finite and fallen creatures, we are all subject to error. We can never be absolutely certain we have not misunderstood an issue, or even God's word. We should never overlook the distinction between scriptural infallibility and human fallibility, since our interpretations and applications are never infallible. To confuse scriptural infallibility with human fallibility robs us of our ability to work with other Christians or with people in general. James Sire wrote: 'As we read Scripture, practice it, live in community with other believers and involve ourselves in worship, we grow, change our minds, modify our theology. Even what we learned yesterday needs to be subject to change as we check it out on the nerve endings of our life and as we hear our friends comment on our insights'.

This isn't an argument for indecisiveness or for a subjective, ever-changing theology. It's an acknowledgement that we may be wrong on many of the complex matters we have to face in modern society, and we may have to modify our opinions. Our authority is still Scripture, but where Scripture does not point unequivocally in one direction, we have to take seriously Christian tradition, the contributions of contemporary Christian thinkers, and even debate within society. And all these insights need to be informed by the Holy Spirit.

Some disagree. For them Christian tradition alone is correct, so that when our culture disagrees, it is inevitably incorrect. For example, some argue that there is a danger in allowing debate on abortion in Christian publications. This is based on the view that abortion is seriously wrong by biblical standards, that it is a departure from 'the accepted views', that 'new' positions ought not to be promoted as guidance for other people to follow, and that 'new moral positions' are accommodations to cultural change. The outcome of such criticism is that it is only 'traditional moral principles' that are worthy of consideration. By definition, no discussion of abortion is allowable. In these terms, traditional moral principles are, without question or debate, regarded as being totally true to Scripture.

This sounds safe. The true way is known since Christian tradition is correct. Unfortunately, it overlooks one possibility, and this is that Christian tradition may be wrong. It is only when this possibility is accepted that we put ourselves in a position where we can learn from Christians with whom we disagree on a wide range of matters.

The picture painted by those who criticize any deviation from Christian tradition is that Christian understanding is unchanging. According to this perspective, there is nothing new in theology or in theological understanding. One has to ask whether such a stance can be taken seriously. Has nothing changed since the early church? Were all today's perspectives worked out at that time, and do we owe nothing to the early church Fathers, to the Reformation, to the evangelical awakenings of the eighteenth century, or to the more modern emphases on the work of the Holy Spirit? If it is argued that these signified a return to the purity of the New Testament, one can then turn to the developments that ushered in the abolition of slavery, that led to the emancipation of women and the protection of young working children, and that brought about the modern missionary movement. These were movements away from what had been regarded in many countries as Christian tradition. One also has to ask whether the Holy Spirit has nothing more to teach Christians of subsequent generations. Surely, we are far from all-wise or all-obedient.

But aren't those who criticize deviations from Christian tradition criticizing deviations from fundamental moral stances? This may be true. What we must be careful about is choosing which moral issues to hold on to, and ignoring others where we have strayed (perhaps for good reasons) far from traditional positions. What is important is not keeping to, or wandering away from, traditional perspectives, but having good reasons why we advocate certain courses of action rather than others. We are to be subject to the criteria of Scripture, not those of Christian tradition. This doesn't mean we should ignore Christian tradition: we are to bring it as well as contemporary practices before the bar of Scripture.

Dogmatism elevates individualism and downgrades the community. It refuses to accept the pluralism of the evangelical world, let alone the pluralism of society. It insists that agreement on the basic tenets of the faith is insufficient; agreement is also required on complex contemporary issues, whether these be the use of force in keeping peace, economic matters, divorce and re-marriage, the role of women in the church, homosexuality, abortion, euthanasia, or any other issues. Faithful followers of Christ do not agree on any of these applied issues, and to insist otherwise is to impose upon evangelicalism a dogmatism and authoritarianism totally foreign to the life and example of Jesus. As a result, arbitrary cultural norms are imposed on evangelical groups, norms that rapidly come to assume more authority than Scripture, since they are neither derived from Scripture nor subject to it. This is tradition abused, and it's a potent force in leading to controversy.

Freedom of expression

My position has an inevitable end-result: differences of opinion are to be expected within evangelicalism, and we have to learn to cope with such differences. This stems from the importance of freedom of thought within Christian circles.

It's imperative that we learn to distinguish between criticism of ideas, and criticism of the people holding those ideas. Strong disagreement with the views of a fellow-Christian doesn't give us the 'right' to question that person's motives or to assault his or her character and reputation. This is character assassination, based upon the supposed superiority of one person over another. It is the opposite of Christian attitudes of servanthood and humility; it denigrates all that the other person stands for.

We have to learn how to disagree with one another in a positive and supportive way. This is essential for genuine tolerance, by which we can take seriously the sharply conflicting views of another person or group. We need to beware of turning friends into enemies because we cannot agree on everything, and of fragmenting the body of Christ because we are unable to agree on some matter peripheral to the essentials of our faith in Christ. This is schism, no matter how important the matter is in its own right.

All these points can be expressed using a metaphor I've referred to repeatedly, that of the body of Christ (1 Cor. 12:12–31). I've dealt with this in chapter 5, and the only point I want to emphasize here is that of the *diversity* it pictures, in the human body and also in the church. The striking differences between different parts

of the human body, and the special honour bestowed by
God on the unseen and 'less honourable' parts of the
human body, point to the importance of *all* parts of
Christ's body — the church. This diversity and hetero-
geneity ensure that different races, ages, cultures, degrees of learning, abilities, personality types, and
outlooks are all essential for the wholeness of Christ's
body. If this is so, freedom of expression is essential.
Otherwise, much of the body will be destined to silence
and forced obedience, and that is hardly conducive to an
active, well-functioning body — either anatomically or
spiritually.

Within Christian circles the principle of dialogue
based on respect for the other's position and integrity, is
crucial. Whenever this is lost, it is replaced by an
unyielding harsh legalism that is prepared to destroy
people and institutions in order to win a political battle.
Even when confronted by notoriously difficult dilemmas, constructive ways forward are possible for those
who have been redeemed and made new in Christ. This
is one of the outcomes of the new life in Christ, and
should characterize the life of the community of the
redeemed.

Constructive ways forward are based on debate and
serious dialogue. The only alternative are piously-
packaged solutions that have the appearance of providing assured answers, and yet will be ignored by
ordinary Christians when confronted by difficult
choices. These answers are superficial ones; they have
the *appearance* of being correct or acceptable but fail to
deal with the intricacies of the problem. Compare the
promises of an opposition political party in the run-up
to an election, and the policies of that party in power
faced by the reality of the country's finances. The ideal-
ism and the reality may be quite different. Christians
have to beware of being content with idealistic notions
that fail to help people at their point of need.

Debate over complex issues not only has a place
within evangelicalism, it is essential for the health of the

evangelical community. There's no other way of tackling issues over which no evangelical consensus has been reached. The presentation of representative evangelical viewpoints is the essence of any community based upon a belief in the priesthood of all believers. If this right of presentation is not safeguarded in the Christian community, we have chosen dictatorship and have lost any semblance of the freedom and responsibility that are found in Christ alone (Gal. 3:1–4:11; 4:21–5:1). Intellectual honesty and spiritual integrity are basic ingredients of a Christian community, and are integral to the moral burden placed upon us as Christ's representatives.

Difficult as it may be to allow, and even encourage, freedom of expression, it is made possible by the Christian's ultimate belief in the triumph of truth over error. This is integral to the hope of the church, stemming as it does from Christ's triumph over death. We are made free in Christ and are to express this freedom in our relationship with others, supremely with other Christians. Inevitably, there are dangers: we may misuse this freedom and exploit it, or we may impose rules as a means of ensuring safety (Gal. 5:13–18). Despite these dangers, we cannot ignore it. To do so is to turn our backs on one of God's richest blessings.

Let's imagine the principal of a school.

She wishes to change certain important aspects of the structure of the school, including introducing alterations to the grouping of subjects, providing far more options for students, and extending the number of staff involved in management of the school. She would like to establish some as group coordinators who would act with her in constituting a creative think-tank. The principal could go about this restructuring task in various ways. She could tell the staff that this is what will happen in future. Or she could introduce the ideas first to a select group of senior staff, in a spirit of advising them that this is what will be happening. A third approach would see her producing a discussion document, in which the ideas plus her reasoning behind them were put forward fully and explicitly. The document would then be openly discussed, so that its merits could be examined in detail; but also allowing for the concerns of staff to be enunciated, and for it to be rejected by the staff if they felt that its disadvantages outweighed its advantages.

These three approaches demonstrate the contrast between an authoritarian approach and one allowing, and welcoming, the opinions and expressions of others. Only the third accepts that freedom of expression has a legitimate place to play in the school environment. The second approach is just as authoritarian as the first, although it has been given a veneer of consultation. Although I have cast the illustration in a secular environment, it applies just as forcibly to any specifically Christian institution. No matter what the environment, it is only the third approach that looks for the contribution (wisdom) of others, that seeks assistance, and that believes in dialogue. It is only this approach that believes that disagreement can be used positively, and that everyone is to be treated as of sufficient value that their opinions and perhaps fears are to be taken seriously. The third way can sometimes be an exceedingly taxing and demanding way. Nevertheless, it is the only way that has any chance of leading to growth in mutual understanding within an organization or community.

Censorship

This is the converse of freedom of expression. It's an unwillingness to allow ideas contrary to one's own to stand the test of public opinion, and is an attempt to protect those holding one's own viewpoint from exposure to conflicting ideas. The motives of the censor may be exemplary, but the result is likely to be a narrow, bigoted constituency.

In Christian terms the need to screen out material with which one disagrees, including material emanating from fellow-believers, is a denial that evangelical faith is consistent either with intellectual freedom or intellectual creativity. It asserts that we are unable to contend for the faith, and that we lack the resources for distinguishing good from evil. I want to argue the opposite: Christians are to believe in intellectual freedom because the person redeemed by Christ has been set free and liberated by the gospel, and can trust in God's sovereignty and direction. Nothing is beyond the scope of God's concern and all human endeavour is under the providence of God. Since it is our minds that have been liberated, we need never fear the truth because our thinking is now carried out within the framework of God's truth. We can face head-on the confused array of contemporary beliefs, analyse them and their presuppositions, and respond with compassion and understanding.

We've been created as thinking creatures. It behoves us, therefore, to indulge in serious thinking, and to decide in a responsible manner what to read and view. This isn't a matter of simply reading and viewing what we agree with, but whatever is a worthy indicator of the thinking and attitudes of the society in which God has placed us — even if we strongly disagree with some of the contents. Our responsibility as Christians is to be faithful representatives of God within society, but this is impossible if we are uninformed about that society. We need to be people who are open and are constructively grappling with the issues of real life as reflected in print, film and art. We are to relish the challenge of all facets of society and its ideas.

If we acknowledge that all truth is God's truth, we should be confident in the ultimate victory of that truth. As God's people, we are to be agents for intellectual freedom. We should be life-affirming people, able to live with a wide range of ideas and concepts, even with those with which we have little sympathy. This demands responsibility and judgement; it also demands a willingness to live with controversy, inside and outside the Christian community.

As long as we have a carefully thought-through world-view, conflicting world-views can be approached with integrity. The intellectual freedom that Christians enjoy seeks to bring all ideas under the scrutiny of God, and all thoughts under the lordship of Christ. In no sense are these new ideas. They were expressed in 1644 by John Milton when he reacted to an ordinance passed by Parliament in 1643 calling for the licensing of the press. The basis of his opposition to censorship was the nature of truth. He wrote: 'Truth is strong, next to the Almighty. She needs no policies, nor strategies, nor licencings to make her victorious — those are the shifts and the defences that error uses against her power. Give her but room, and do not bind her when she sleeps, for then she speaks not true'.

In the end truth will triumph over error, even if error appears to be victorious in the short-term. But how can we recognize truth, since it is so often mixed with error? James Sire has commented: 'In a fallen world the possibility of error is the necessary condition for the entrance and triumph of truth'. The two have to be seen together; they have to be compared and stand up to criticism. Again, it was Milton who wrote: 'Assuredly we bring not innocence into the world, we bring impurity much rather: that which purifies us is trial, and trial is by what is contrary. That virtue therefore which . . . knows not the utmost that vice promises to her followers, and rejects it, is but a blank virtue, not a pure'.

If we accept these arguments, the conclusion we have to draw is that there is no room for censorship within Christian circles, where access to all kinds of thinking is essential. Otherwise, we shall foster a community in which people are unable to encounter opposition of any kind. In the long-term censorship fosters weakness and not strength, and that is not the way of Christ's kingdom.

This is fine, you may say, but what about children, surely they should be protected from evil and pernicious ideas? What about those who, while not children, are easily led and are weak — they too should be protected for their own good? What about those who, while neither children nor weak, claim to be committed to an institution (say a church or a denominational Bible College) but say or do things that are against the basic rules of that institution; surely we have a duty to stop them going their own way? Let me explain. Children and the weak do require the protection of society, but not under the guise of censorship. Protection takes many forms, generally requires the support of laws and, frequently, of parents or guardians. It has to be readily enforceable. Censorship *per se* rarely accomplishes this, and too much should not be expected of it.

To argue against too easy a resort to censorship, as I have done, is not the same as allowing everything. It doesn't allow people to drive at any speed they like on public roads, it doesn't mean every conceivable book or video (regardless of literary or artistic merit) should be made available in every public library, and it doesn't mean that Bible College lecturers can teach atheism. There are strictures, but these are based on clear guiding principles, whether they be ones to do with road safety, literary standards, or central Christian beliefs. Such strictures can be applied even by those who are implicitly committed to freedom of expression and the responsibility of individual decision-making. There is a major gulf between attitudes which only restrict liberty as a last resort, and those that actively seek to protect individuals from the dangers of 'improper' beliefs or attitudes and that regard censorship as a crucial weapon in this battle.

Second, censorship can be applied to enforce diametrically opposing beliefs, ideas and practices. Just as it can be used to enforce strict moral standards, it can also be employed to make liberal standards the norm. It can be used in support of Christianity, but just as readily it can be used against Christianity. It can be used to legitimize evangelical beliefs; it can be used to promulgate liberal theological positions, or many forms of atheism. Censorship reflects the ethos of those doing the censoring.

Third, great care has to be taken to ensure that censorship does not degenerate into a means by which individuals exert power over others. This applies particularly to a situation where an institution is dependent upon the money of a single individual. Not unnaturally, this individual wishes to see his money put to 'good' use, that is, a use of which he approves. Difficulties ensue where the beliefs of those employed by the institution begin to differ from those of the philanthropist, perhaps not in fundamental ways, but sufficiently to cause the philanthropist to want them removed. All too easily conflict arises, where the quest for power (by the philanthropist) and the freedom of expression (of the staff members) are pitted against one another. Censorship of this type has sinister overtones, and has little to do with the attitudes of Christ.

Censorship in some guises may be inevitable, and yet our bias should always be against it. In practice, every situation has to be assessed on its own merits, and ideological solutions are rarely adequate ones. Censorship is always a last resort.

Helping each other

Polemical writing, hot rhetoric, censorship, a pressure group mentality, individualism, authoritarianism, and loyalty to a political slogan work together to break up the body of Christ. Each of these in its own way is a call for independence, and each of these places an ideal, a goal, or a person above loyalty to Christ. *Independence* is fostered rather than *interdependence*.

We need each other, and so we are to support each other. Not only this, but we have inescapable obligations to each other, namely, to talk to each other: to uphold each other, and to respect each other. As we begin to treat each other like this, we will be in a position to cope with dissenting views within the community of the Lord's people. How do we do this?

In the first place, we are to realize that our brothers and sisters in Christ are indeed precisely that, whatever there may be that divides us. They are, in Donald MacKay's words, 'front-line comrades', whose chief end in life is to glorify God and enjoy him for ever. What is true of us is also true of fellow-believers, for whom Christ died, who are earnestly seeking to be faithful as Christians, even if there are issues that separate us.

Implicit in this is a second set of obligations: we are to listen to each other, seeking to understand and appreciate what others are stressing. We are to seek that which is genuinely Christ-affirming in their position, however much we may disagree with the interpretation or practical outcome. Under no circumstances are we to caricature the views of a fellow-believer, or insist that a fellow-Christian is lying, being a hypocrite, or guilty of foul motives. We are to be faithful to each other by expressing accurately and fairly those viewpoints with which we disagree. And of course, we are to talk to one another, discuss frankly our differences and the reasons for them, and assess our own faithfulness and the nature of our own views. Together we are to seek that which is true in each position, and then affirm these truths.

Third, we are to help and encourage each other, even when we differ on issues we think are of considerable importance. This is necessary because we are engaged in a common enterprise, that of forwarding the cause of Christ and of being his faithful representatives in a pluralist society. We do it by providing feedback for the others, through carefully thought through criticism of their position. This includes raising serious questions which they may not have asked, and which may help to throw additional light on the validity or otherwise of their position. In the same way, we are to be prepared to have our own position questioned and challenged. It can only occur in an atmosphere of mutual support, seeking each other's good and together seeking the mind of Christ.

Fourth, we are to meet each other face to face. This is ideal; it is not always possible. When impossible, we should write to each other rather than harangue each other in public. We should let each other know informally what we think, and not immediately criticize and condemn publicly. To meet each other or, at least, to correspond, is to begin seeing each other as real people, especially as fellow-believers. We begin appreciating the others as human beings, not simply as public faces. We begin to see them as they are before God, and not as representatives of a rival evangelical constituency. They are people for whom we are to pray, and for whose well-being we are to strive.

As we love them as human beings, we become concerned for them. Even if we think they are on the verge of heresy, we are to commit ourselves to support and aid them, not score points off them in a debate or heresy trial. The others may be wrong and may need our assistance; but we also may be wrong and may need their assistance. Mutual interdependence is crucial, and informally and quietly meeting with one another, face to face, is a vital prerequisite.

In the fifth place, the assistance of other Christians is frequently of enormous help when differences separate us. When we think someone is guilty of a serious error, we should solicit the advice of others, especially those who are knowledgeable in the area of concern, before acting or reacting publicly. Dialogue is essential and is the most important means for determining truth in a world where truth is entwined with error. Not one of us possesses the final truth, however much we may be tempted to think that we do. It may sound provocative, but it is fundamental for Christians. Mutual interdependence is not an optional extra for a Christian community; it is fundamental to its integrity.

Questions for group discussion

1. How easy have you found it to ask questions about difficult topics in your church? Discuss your experiences. How have you responded?

2. Comment on the two churches in the 'Pressure groups' section. Think how you would have responded in the same situation. Can you think of other (more realistic) examples?

3. Discuss the place of Christian tradition in our lives as Christians today. How do you decide whether it is helpful or not?

4. Do you think it is unwise to emphasize Christians' freedom of expression as much as is done in this chapter? Discuss its dangers and benefits.

5. Discuss the pros and cons of censorship.

6. Outline some ways in which we can support one another within the church.

SEVEN

Where Should Lines Be Drawn?

Central or peripheral?

Let us imagine a church — we shall call it church M —
that has become embroiled with the question of homosexuality. The issue has come to a head on account of the
church's relationship with a neighbouring church
(church P), the minister of which is known to be a
practising homosexual. He has made it widely known
that this is his lifestyle, and he considers his stand to be
a legitimate expression of Christian discipleship.

How should the leadership of church M respond?
Should they, as they have done in the past, take part in
local ecumenical activities, knowing that these involve
church P and its openly homosexual minister? Or should
they sever all relations with church P, letting the minister
know that this stems from his avowedly homosexual
lifestyle, telling him to repent and pleading with him to
give up what church M considers to be a sinful lifestyle?

While the leadership is considering this, some within
the church community are demanding clear statements
on where church M stands on homosexuality. They want
to know whether the church leadership would allow a
homosexual into membership, and if so whether any

distinction would be made between a person with a homosexual orientation (but who is not a practising homosexual) and a person having an overt homosexual relationship with one or more partners. They also want to know whether any present members of the church are homosexuals, and if so they demand to know what action will be taken against them. Some within the church argue that homosexuality automatically separates a person from God, and that it is impossible to be a homosexual (it isn't always clear how this designation is being used) and a Christian.

The leadership of church M has problems with some of these pressures, since, while not condoning homosexual behaviour, they consider that the 'sin of homosexuality' should never be totally isolated from many other sins — including ones that are tolerated within their own church community. They also wish to approach those with a homosexual orientation (and possibly behaviour) in a pastoral manner; they want to assure them of God's love and grace, and show them the place of repentance and renewal in Christ. While they have no desire to justify homosexual practice, they have considerable reservations over whether public condemnation of homosexuals and homosexuality is the biblical approach. They are also extremely concerned because this particular issue is dividing the church; some who are clamouring for precise statements on homosexuality have already said they will leave the church if the leadership does not act in the ways they are requesting.

The problems presented by this scenario are considerable. It is not my intention to explore homosexuality as such, and I shall not attempt to provide any guidelines for a church such as the one depicted here. That is for others to determine. What does concern me is the over-all approach adopted to a situation such as this one. Where are lines to be drawn? Is the question of homosexuality a central one for the Christian church or is it a peripheral one? What are the options?

I'm using homosexuality as an illustration of the type of issues that pose real problems for Christian churches (and para-church groups). I could have used any number of other illustrations. However, homosexuality seems to me to be a good one, since it tenuously straddles the divide between central and peripheral matters, and is an issue of very real concern for many Christian groups at the present time.

In terms of homosexuality (or any comparable issue) I recognize four options open to Christians. For the sake of this discussion, I shall work on the assumption that the biblical ideal is that sexual relationships are to be expressed within a permanent, monogamous heterosexual union, and that homosexual expression deviates from this biblical ideal.

A *first option* is that homosexuality is regarded as a peripheral matter, and as such it doesn't matter too much what position Christians adopt. This applies whatever peripheral issue is under discussion. According to this stance, rigid lines have to be drawn over central matters, but with peripheral matters a different approach should be adopted. An *alternative option* is that homosexuality is regarded as a peripheral matter, but that biblical principles are seen to be as relevant to it as they are to central concerns. There are biblically drawn limits and there are biblical principles, and a point may come where separation from other Christians is necessitated. However, since homosexuality is not at the core of Christian concerns, the reasons leading to separation must be very strong ones, and in all probability this will only occur in extreme circumstances. A *third possibility* is that, although homosexuality is regarded as a peripheral question, it is of such importance that in practice it should be viewed as if it were central. Hence, according to this position, it is appropriate to lay down rigid rules regarding sexual conduct in the church, and to take decisive action against fellow-Christians when these rules are broken. In these terms separation, on the basis of differing viewpoints regarding the significance of homosexual behaviour, is legitimate and is even to be encouraged. A *fourth option* is that homosexuality is regarded as so important that central Christian affirmations should contain statements about sexual conduct, and that these terms should leave no place for homosexuality of any description within Christianity as the two are in complete antithesis to one another.

Which option?

Let us look first at the two extreme positions: options one and four. Option four should be dismissed. If an anti-homosexual (homophobic) stance is regarded as central to Christian affirmations, the only conclusion that could be drawn is that conformity to moral norms (however important some of these may be) is as important for Christianity as is Christ's death on the cross. Very readily, the two become confused and the gospel of grace is converted into a gospel of good works and moral rectitude. The gospel also becomes reduced to a one-issue statement; for some, the issue of importance is homosexuality, for others it may be abortion, the sovereignty of God, the manner in which the universe was created, or speaking in tongues. This is not to downgrade any one of these concerns; it is simply to recognize that the gospel soon becomes unrecognizable when any one of these issues is placed on centre stage. All too readily the conclusion is reached that Christianity has no message of hope for those with the 'wrong' viewpoint in these (and other) areas. In my example here, it appears to offer no hope for those with homosexual tendencies, let alone those who overtly practise homosexuality.

The fourth option is an understandable one, since many of these issues are dealt with by the biblical writers. Elevating what I have termed peripheral matters to a place of central concern may reflect a desire to apply biblical principles as widely and consistently as possible across all areas of life. It is a worthy goal, but is this the most appropriate way to achieve such a worthy objective?

Making a subsidiary concern into a central one will undoubtedly highlight the issue in question, but at what cost? If particular sexual behaviour patterns are stressed to such an extent that Christianity becomes intimately associated with these patterns, and at odds with any other patterns, Christians will stand out on these grounds and perhaps on these grounds alone. Where, then, does the offer of salvation in Christ enter the equation? What do Christians have to offer those who fail to live up to the standards we so publicly and vigorously espouse? It may be that some will respond to the gospel and repent of their previous lifestyle, and that is to be welcomed. Nevertheless, undue concern with a particular lifestyle may itself place in jeopardy the wholeness and all-embracing nature of the gospel. One way in which this becomes evident is when a variety of Christian groups, all with single-issue concerns, rub shoulders. Some of their concerns will be mutually exclusive, and the problems of the situation then becomes all too obvious.

The other extreme position is option one. It says that because an issue such as homosexuality is peripheral, it doesn't matter too much what we believe or how we act: after all, this is *only* a peripheral area. According to this option, the sexual behaviour of Christians is irrelevant: anything goes. I put it at the other extreme because it denies that there are any biblical data relevant to areas such as these. This position fails to appreciate that God is concerned with every aspect of life, and hence it has major repercussions for our view of God and of the nature of Christ's redeeming work on the cross. It also questions the nature of the biblical revelation, since the biblical writers touch on all aspects of human experience and relationships. No realm of our lives remains untouched by the concerns of God and by the consequences of Christ's death and resurrection.

What it demonstrates is that the division of our concerns into central and peripheral ones is artificial. For many practical purposes it's useful to make this distinction. However, God does not put more emphasis on the one than on the other. Nothing is too small or too insignificant to be the object of his attention and care. The central/peripheral distinctions must not blur this important point. We must beware of ignoring peripheral issues because of our stress on central issues, just as we dare not elevate peripheral issues until, in effect, they overshadow central ones.

The biblical framework is all-embracing, and so biblical principles can never be overlooked when confronted by peripheral concerns, no matter how open to dispute they may be. All our approaches and all our attitudes are to be illuminated by biblical insights. Option one is no option.

More options

This leaves options two and three. Both options take biblical teaching seriously and consider it relevant to questions such as homosexuality. Proponents of both positions are attempting to apply biblical perspectives to all aspects of life and want to approach matters Christianly. They differ on the degree to which they think that biblical patterns can be applied to society as a whole, or even to those within the Christian community who interpret biblical teaching differently. Those adhering to option two allow considerable flexibility for points of view other than their own, even when they strongly disagree with some of these viewpoints. By contrast, those espousing option three tend to regard their own interpretation of Scripture as the only acceptable one, and so will be far more ready to separate from those with conflicting perspectives.

Option three people elevate matters like homosexuality to the centre of Christianity, treating them virtually on a par with central doctrinal issues. This occurs even when they concede that such matters are peripheral ones, and are not strictly speaking essential to Christian belief. However, once this is done, the end-result is little different from that of the option four group, for whom major controversy is to be expected over many issues, regardless of whether they are classed as central or peripheral. Once all controlling distinction is lost between central and peripheral matters, the ability to handle the consequences of differences of opinion is also lost.

This leaves option two, which I regard as fulfilling the essential provisos. It accepts Biblical principles as exerting a controlling influence over all areas of life, and it accepts a hierarchy of concerns within the Christian community. Within this hierarchy, no issues are regarded as unimportant, and yet all issues are not given equal prominence. No area lies outside the scope of God's concern, and yet battles are not to be fought indiscriminately. The result of this approach is that Christians do not separate from each other simply because they disagree on certain matters. What is crucial is the nature of the matters in question, rather than how firmly we feel about them, or how strongly we are convinced that our position accords with biblical teaching. Option two allows different opinions on many issues within the Christian community, but it continues to hold to the importance of the essentials. Any separation from other Christians must only occur in the most extreme of circumstances, and on the most crucial of issues.

Single-issue divisions

The illustration I've just considered, highlights some of the problems we encounter when discussion is confined to a single issue. The members of the congregation of church M who were prepared to leave the church over this question were elevating this one issue (no matter how important in its own right) above all others. They were prepared to leave even if they agreed with the church's leadership on all crucial doctrinal questions regarding the person and work of Christ, the nature of the church, and the meaning of Christian discipleship. For them, this one issue had taken precedence over all others.

Let's imagine that some people did leave the church. What then? What other church would they feel able to become aligned with? One imagines it would have to be a church holding exactly the same position as the one they held on homosexuality. Assuming that they found a local church like this, what other strictures would they impose? Would it have to be of the same denomination as church M? Would it have to hold the same position on baptism, church government, and the gifts of the Spirit? Would it have to hold to the same central Christian doctrines? What if it belonged to a denomination that allowed diverse views on homosexuality?

The possibilities are endless. When single issues are elevated, considerable problems follow if attempts are made to be consistent. It's all too easy to focus on the one issue in question, and have little interest in other, equally important issues. This makes life manageable, but fails to encourage biblical thinking and practice. One specific issue has become the touchstone of all decisions and aspirations, so that faithfulness to the gospel is measured by the one issue in question.

Whenever this is the case, fundamental questions need to be asked about the role of the church, including the local church where these issues are being debated. What is the purpose of the church? Where does the particular single issue that is creating the problems, fit in? What would we like the church to be remembered for in, say, 50 years' time?

What are we looking for in the overall ministry of a church? Is it a biblically-based ministry, a Christ-centred ministry, and one where we and others receive help in understanding the Scriptures? Or are we seeking to receive direction in political matters, be told how to vote, be provided with answers on social issues, and take part in social campaigns? While these two

approaches may not be mutually exclusive, they tend to
represent quite different philosophies. The first emphasizes the importance of a biblical understanding of the
world and God's purposes, so that in the light of this
understanding Christians can frame their responses to
problems in society. The second relies far more on
responses already formulated by certain church leaders,
responses that are then provided ready-made for other
Christians to accept and act upon. The judgements of
the leaders are transferred to their followers, who may
or may not appreciate the reasons behind them.

What is of supreme importance to a church? Is it
conformity to moral norms (however important some of
these may be), or is it oneness in Christ and learning to
accept differences of opinion on peripheral issues?
Those who stress the place of peripheral issues or moral
statements within the church, have little to say about
learning to accept others who are not like us in one way
or another. What matters to them is conformity to a
particular statement, rather than understanding those
who do not wish to have anything to do with it. The
political platform mentality has major repercussions for
the life of a local church, and inevitably clouds the
centrality of Christ and the thrust of the gospel.

Pastoral implications

What are the pastoral implications of undue emphasis
on a strict view regarding an issue such as homosexuality? If, as in the illustration I've used, some Christians
demand a precise stance on homosexual orientation as
well as behaviour, numerous pastoral considerations are
raised. What is known about the sexual practices of
leaders of any church, including one's own? What is
known about the sexual practices (let alone thoughts) of
church members? How much do we know about the
anger, dissension, untruthfulness, and envy in their
lives? Do we split from other churches on these grounds,

and do we exclude from membership all who fail on these grounds? Even to suggest that such actions be taken (except in the most extreme of circumstances), would be akin to approving of an inquisitorial witch-hunt of the secret thoughts of all church members. Such churches exist; the one feature they have in common is reckless disregard of the teaching and example of Jesus.

To return to my illustration, those who wish to adopt a hard-line stance against the openly homosexual minister of church P, have to face up to what their response would be to another church (church R) with a divorced (and remarried) minister (which they consider is contrary to Christ's teaching). Would they respond in the same way, especially if the divorce and remarriage had taken place while this other minister was a Christian? He may even advocate the appropriateness of these actions, and may officiate at weddings of divorced Christians. In every other area, they admit, his preaching is biblical and his lifestyle exemplary.

I'm not suggesting there are no differences between the ministers of churches P and R. I'm not suggesting that the actions of both should not be very carefully scrutinized. What I am suggesting is that enormous care has to be exercised as to the appropriate responses to these issues, and that forthright condemnation of the one, but not the other shows a disconcerting lack of consistency. This is the hallmark of all single-issue approaches.

The trouble with a single-issue approach is that any one issue can be singled out as a concern and become the focal point of attention. What if the minister of the other church had been female (and we considered this unbiblical)? Should all connections with this other church be cut off, and should the minister be asked to repent and resign from the ministry? What if the other minister was an extremely difficult person to get on with, and there was evidence that he was devious in his dealings with people in his church and appeared to be living in comparative luxury at the expense of his congregation? Or again, what if the minister's wife had had an abortion, and we disapproved of this? What if he occasionally drank too much alcohol and had been convicted of drunk driving? Where does one draw the line along this path? Are some of these peripheral issues more important than others, so that different principles should be used in different situations? What would Christ have done?

What if the openly homosexual minister was the minister of one's own church (church M) rather than of a neighbouring church? A primary consideration here is whether one joined the church knowing this to be the situation, and why a minister known to be a practising homosexual was invited to become minister. It is unlikely that this situation would arise without warning, and that in turn raises questions about the nature of the church in question. If a practising homosexual is the minister, what does this tell the congregation about the minister's approach to Scripture, to interpersonal relationships, to homosexuality in general, and to marriage? Does it have any consequences for his own relationship with members of the church? Does he advocate a homosexual lifestyle as part of his ministry? Similar questions have to be asked if the minister has a homosexual orientation, but is celibate. Questions such as these are pertinent in helping to decide what action to take, just as they would be if the minister had an unsatisfactory marriage, was a poor father, was an evolutionist (for church members who were scientific creationists), was pro-choice (when many in the church were ardently pro-life), or was postmillenial (for church members who were premillenial).

My aim is not to attempt to provide specific answers. However, I can conceive a situation where, for the good of the church as a community, the minister was asked to leave, or where church members felt they had to leave. Either course of action should only arise where the gospel appeared to be at stake, and where the message being given to those outside the church was contrary to the reconciliation and hope we have in Christ. However, any such action should only be taken after every means of forgiveness has been tried and has failed. Separation and division may come, but this end-result demonstrates failure of understanding (and perhaps lack of relationship with Christ) somewhere within the warring factions.

Am I making matters too complex?

Some may say that there is a difference in responsibilities between an ordinary Christian and one in the role of a Christian teacher or Christian author. The latter have responsibilities towards churches, Christian institutions and Christian publishers to teach the truth, guard against error, and protect the vulnerable. The thrust of this criticism is that my emphases fail to take seriously such distinctions.

I am more than willing to agree that any teacher carries considerable responsibilities, and that any Christian church or para-church organization has great responsibility in teaching the truth, guarding against error, and protecting the vulnerable. How is it best accomplished?

First, let me be negative. It is not accomplished by censorship and judgementalism, as I have already argued. Biblical Christianity shouldn't display any hint of this mentality. Neither should we treat the majority of Christians as children, who cannot be trusted to think issues through Christianly, and who have to be led every step of the way. Undoubtedly, there are Christians like this, and new Christians inevitably go through such a stage in their spiritual development. But to accept that this is where most Christians remain, is to accept a far lower standard than Paul, who worked hard to ensure that the Christians at Corinth (1 Cor. 3:1–3) moved from a diet of spiritual milk to one of spiritual meat. To accept that most evangelical Christians never grow up spiritually and have to be continually provided with a diet of simple answers to complex issues, is to accept a sub-biblical framework.

Still on the negative side, Christian teachers should not restrict themselves to didactic teaching methods. Successful education, whatever area it is in, stimulates students to go on and learn for themselves, building on their understanding, and rejoicing in what they achieve. For Christians, 'self-directed learning' is biblically-based and Spirit-directed. Without it, there can be no growth in spiritual understanding, which includes commitment to truth as opposed to falsehood, spiritually-discerned judgement rather than carnal analysis, and Christ-centred motives instead of self-serving ambition.

What, then, of the positive side? Responsibility is to be taken seriously. For Christians this means being true to the triune God — God the Father, God the Son, and God the Holy Spirit — rather than being limited to any human organization, whether denomination, local church, or para-church organization. Our highest authority must always be Christ as we seek to work things out in terms of biblical principles and guidelines.

It will protect us from stating simply what certain Christian pressure groups may or may not want us to state. To put forward the status quo on any issue, because this is what our peers wish us to put forward, is to fail in our highest duty — our duty to Christ. There are limits to the views we can express, but these are set by biblical guidelines and not by the interpretations of certain Christians. There may well be differences of opinion, but they will be within the broad framework of a biblical approach. This is where the responsibility of the Christian teacher, speaker, and author comes into play — it exposes people to a biblically-based and serious Christian interpretation, rather than personal perspectives.

This leads on to the second positive point, namely,

Christian leaders, churches, and organizations have a responsibility to teach the truth, but on the type of matters I have been dealing with where the truth itself may not be obvious, what then, should be taught?

The goal of all teaching should be to assist Christians in determining how best to approach issues, working out what biblical principles are relevant (and what are not), and finding the best way to help those struggling with these issues. Remember, my concern is with disputable issues, and the 'truth' may be more in a correct approach than in a correct answer (since the correct answer may vary from one Christian to another). Guarding against error may entail guarding against erroneous and misleading approaches, and the vulnerable may actually be protected by gaining insight into the contradictions of the different approaches adopted by different Christians. Of course, issues aren't always this complex, but the type of issues I've been discussing too often are. To suggest otherwise is to mislead, and to mislead is never the way of Christ. It is dishonest and devious, far removed from the Christian way.

It is unlikely that a five-page analysis of a horrendously difficult issue can ever provide anyone with all they need to know about the issue. It may be a helpful summary, and, for many Christians, it may be all they need; there is nothing wrong in that. But to suggest that a five-page summary is all there is to be known about the issue is nonsense. This should never be the stance of Christians, to whom the truth is of supreme importance.

Knowing where to draw lines

We are to be committed to what we believe. We are to be so committed to the truths of the Christian gospel that we live them out in our own lives, we want others to see their reality for themselves, and we are prepared to strive for the truth we recognize in Christianity. We hold our beliefs with tenacity. Nothing I have written should be interpreted as a half-hearted commitment to the central truths of the Christian faith. However, holding one's beliefs with tenacity is not the same as being arrogant and rude towards others. At all times we are to be courteous as well as firm, gracious while we strive for our own position, and loving even to those we consider as mistaken.

More than this, *all* our beliefs are to be held in this manner, both those we (and others) consider as crucial to the Christian position, and those we consider as peripheral and open to dispute. There is no place for a woolly uncertainty over any of our beliefs. We *are* to contend for the Christian faith, not only for the significance of the work of Christ on the cross but also for whatever position we regard as biblical on baptism or homosexuality. However, hard-headed contention like this is *not* the same as cajoling opponents into an acceptance of *our* positions.

All our beliefs are to be held with openness as well as with commitment and tenacity. We may be mistaken; perhaps our perspective is a blinkered one. We are to enter into dialogue with others, whether these be evangelical Christians of another persuasion from our own, Christians with a liberal theological position, materialists, agnostics, scientific humanists, or Muslims. But what does this imply?

Let's imagine a scale ranging from 100 to 0. Towards the upper end of the scale (the '100'-end) are beliefs considered central to biblical Christianity. Towards the lower end of the scale (the '0'-end) are the peripheral and disputable issues. Between the two ends there will be a continuum, so that some central issues may be ranked at, let us say, 60 to 100. The same would apply to the peripheral issues (perhaps 10 to 40 for many of them). In the middle (at around 50), there may well be overlap between what some groups consider as central and other groups consider as peripheral. What is important is not where various issues are placed on this scale, but that we are open on all issues, and are far more convinced of the truth of those beliefs higher up the scale than of those lower down it. In other words, we will be far less willing to compromise on those issues towards the top end of the scale, although we will always be willing to discuss them with doubters.

Using this scale, we will draw lines and will ardently defend those truths towards the upper end of the scale. We will recognize these as essential for any form of biblical Christianity. We may still admit that our understanding of some details is partial, but we won't doubt that they are central to the biblical revelation. We will hold these beliefs with passion and vigour, and we will be prepared to stand up vigorously for them.

The same cannot be said of those towards the lower end of the scale, although we may still recognize that important biblical truths are at stake. These are not irrelevant, and we may be prepared to stand up for some of them in society and even before other biblical Christians. However, they are open to dispute, even among fellow-believers, and we will be aware of our limited understanding. We will be more prepared to change our opinions on these matters, and we will enjoy dialogue with others (especially with other Christians) over them.

There is more. Truth is not simply an intellectual phenomenon. While truth is to be understood, it is also to be internalized: it is to become part of what we *are* as people. All our beliefs as Christians are to influence how we live, how we respond to others, the way we love others, and the concern we demonstrate for the welfare of others. We are to *be* the people of God. This reminds us that the issues I've been discussing take us far beyond the 'rights' and 'wrongs' of doctrinal statements alone. We *are* to contend for the truth, but this is more than an abstract truth about some belief or other (no matter how important the belief). We are to contend for the truth in ways that will convince others by what we *are* as people. There's no virtue in winning a debate on an issue (whether Christ's saving work on the cross, or creationism) and then demonstrating by the poor quality of *our lives*, that what we have won is only a political battle.

Once we accept this, we begin to appreciate that agreement on the niceties of every issue (especially those at the lower end of my scale) is unnecessary. Within Christian circles, there should be agreement on general (biblical) principles, but their detailed outworking may be open to considerable debate. Christian individuals and groups may express beliefs differently, but they should agree on foundation principles and should internalize these principles in their own lives and relationships with others, that is, they should be 'one in the truth'. On the other hand, those who agree on the details of an issue but have not internalized what they believe, may fail to demonstrate these principles by what they are as people.

My final point is a provocative one: it should be possible to devise a test for the rightness or wrongness of our attitudes. We should be able to disagree with people fervently, and at the same time respect them, be courteous to them, show concern for them as people (and also as fellow-Christians), be happy in their company, and be active in praying for them. In other words, we should be able to hold our beliefs (central or peripheral) with passion, but still be able to talk to those with whom we disagree, pray for and with them, enjoy their company, and even laugh and cry with them. If we fail this test, we have failed to adopt biblical attitudes.

If we are prepared to destroy others for the sake of our beliefs (central or peripheral), we have drawn lines in the wrong places. The same applies if we are prepared to separate from others without a great deal of prayer and study. The latter may take place (especially over central beliefs — towards the top end of my scale), but our respect for others and hopefully theirs for us, must remain intact. There is a chance this may happen as we *live out* the truth, but there is no chance of it occurring if we ignore the attitudes we see in the life and example of Jesus.

Lines are to be drawn; central issues (towards the top end of the scale) are to be contended for passionately; peripheral issues (towards the lower end of the scale) are to be argued through tenaciously and firmly, knowing that our grasp of the issues may be limited. But all this is to take place with courteous proclamation of the truth (central issues) and respectful dialogue (on peripheral issues). In all this, the quality of our lives, our *being* Christian and having Christ-like attitudes, are to govern and control every debate and controversy in which we are involved.

Questions for group discussion

1. Imagine you are one of the leaders of church M in the illustration. How would you attempt to guide the church in this situation?

2. Can you describe any situation in which you have been involved where division has occurred or been threatened? How did you respond, and what have you learned from the incident?

3. As a church member, how do you view your pastor (minister, vicar)? What are your expectations of him/her? How critical are you of his/her failings? Give examples of her/his characteristics that concern and possibly alarm you. What have you done about them?

4. Using the '0–100' scale, list beliefs/attitudes/issues that you would rate towards the top end of the scale, and those you would rate towards the lower end. Compare lists, and discuss those over which there is disagreement.

5. 'Truth is not simply an intellectual phenomenon. While truth is to be understood, it is also to be internalized: it is to become part of what we *are* as people.' Do you agree with this statement? Discuss whether you recognize a tension between *believing* and *being*.

EIGHT

The Enjoyment of Difference

Life in Lifdyl

Let's imagine we are living in a world with quite a different level of technological development from the one we now inhabit. In this world of our imaginings (let's call it Lifdyl), when we travel along motorways the minimum speed is 70 mph, because cars have been designed to travel no slower than this. This is their absolute base speed. For a variety of reasons some Christians consider this is the only acceptable speed at which cars should be allowed to travel, although other Christians are prepared to accept speeds of up to 75 mph. The first group is convinced that the only way to be truly Christian and to be faithful to their interpretation of the Bible is to stick rigidly to the slowest speed possible. Any deviation from this is an accommodation to the inroads of secular Lifdylian influences with their desire for ever-increasing speeds. The second group of Christians has given the matter serious thought and considers that, while this slightly higher speed has more risks associated with it, it too reflects important Christian attitudes. The majority of others in Lifdyl (including a few Christians) regularly travel up to 120 mph; people such as these consider that even though there are safety problems at these higher speeds, other factors also have to be taken into account, such as the desire to have more time for business meetings and family gatherings. Yet others are even less fastidious and travel, on some occasions, as fast as 200 mph, very close to the limit cars can bear and which frequently has tragic consequences.

The Christians who travel between 70 and 75 mph are agreed in rejecting the arguments put forward for higher speeds. However, they also encounter great difficulty in accepting each others' positions. Those who travel at 70 mph consider that those Christians who travel faster than this are failing in their Christian duty, and a minority may even consider they are not true Christians. It is sometimes argued that these 'fast' Christians have sided with those who travel at much higher speeds, and that, in time, they too will increase their travel speeds well beyond 75 mph. They are on a slippery slope (an increasing speed slope in this case) that will end in total rejection of the 70 mph ethos, and which is simply an indication of their incipient unfaithfulness.

On the other side of the argument are those Christians who are prepared to travel up to 75 mph, and who despair of their Christian friends with absolute 70-mph attitudes. They see these attitudes as being unrealistic and unhelpful in a world where most people travel at very much higher speeds, and where clinging to the 70 mph standard isolates Christians from meaningful contact with most other people in Lifdyl. In time these two groups of Christians cease speaking to one another, having overlooked the many things they have in common off the motorway. The difference of 5 mph between the two groups overshadows the fact that they share the 50–80 mph range in their standards and attitudes, radically different to the standards and attitudes of most other Lifdylians.

This unlikely story is a parable, that should neither be interpreted too precisely, nor used to support any of our favourite positions on theological, ethical, or church matters. What it is saying to us is that we have to learn to live with those who are very similar to us on most matters (on major doctrinal and most ethical issues), but who differ from us on certain specific issues they consider essential matters of faith, ethics, and/or biblical interpretation. In other words, it speaks to us about how we cope with those who insist on travelling at speeds different from us on the motorways of Lifdyl.

Parables and problem issues

A parable like this one annoys some people because they think it trivializes important issues. And I can understand why they react in this way. After all, if some particular issue is the most important issue in the world to *me*, I'm going to be indignant at having it compared to something as trivial as speeding. But isn't this the point I've been making throughout this book? Our temptation is to make one issue more important than everything else, even more important than all the things we have in common as Christians. And so, to feel indignant when someone is prepared to compare this all-important matter to cars driving along a motorway at different speeds, demonstrates that it has in fact become too important.

The point of the parable, of course, has nothing what-soever to do with speed limits in a fictitious society. It speaks to those of us who are prepared to separate from others close to us on many important matters but not identical to us (nor we to them). As in all forms of rivalry, we are harshest on those who are most similar to us. We know too much about each other and we expect too much of each other. Those who drive at 75 mph when our own standard insists that nothing more than 70 mph is acceptable, become the objects of our con-demnation and derision, even as we ignore those who keep few of our stipulations and drive at 150 mph. In a similar way, someone committed to postmillenialism may be harshest on a premillenialist. And yet these two have almost everything in common: their shared faith, plus enormous shared interests in prophecy. They have far more in common than what they share with many other Christians who think little about prophecy, and they have infinitely more in common with each other than with secular people who think little about either the Christian faith or prophecy. The trouble is that it's easier to disagree with those with whom we have a great deal in common. Think of neighbouring countries which have shared cultures and backgrounds, and yet love to do battle with each other — verbally, in sport, and sometimes in war. Or political parties that splinter and fragment because one group has broken some hallowed traditional belief of the party.

Perhaps I can be even more facetious and compare the situation to a lettuce salad. No matter how enticing the carrots, spring onions, radishes, lemons, or grapes (add your own delicacies), the foundation is lettuce. What we often seem to do is argue about carrots or radishes, forgetting about the lettuce altogether. How ironic that people who love lettuce salads can spend their time arguing about the additions and the secondary ingredients. Surely, this too is a picture of the church, with its predilection for arguing over subsidiary matters, forgetting what we have in common. Once again, some may be appalled that I can compare what they regard as big issues to lettuce salads, but that is what analogies are all about.

Who are the problem drivers? Is it those who drive at 150 mph, or those who drive at 75 mph? It's obvious what the answer should be for those who are 70-mph drivers, but often this isn't how it works out in practice. And this is true whether the issue at stake is a life-and-death one like euthanasia, or a meaty theological one like women's ordination, or a local church one like the nature of the music at a morning service. Conflict and division arise as easily over church music as over the other two. I have aimed throughout these pages to show that this is not how we should act, no matter how strongly we feel over these or many other secondary issues. Any issue can become a problem issue, if we allow it to.

For many people, a parable like my Lifdyl story raises another problem. It assumes that we are able to think matters through rationally; we are capable of using our minds to cope with the disagreements that divide us. To these people my approach may appear too academic: analysing issues and sorting them out in an unemotional way. For many this is a far cry from the world they inhabit, where people in churches become irate over the colour of the walls in the vestry, the way in which the pastor dresses (is he wearing the same jacket and tie yet again?), the manner in which church business meetings are conducted, or the food at the last missionary fete ('But it wasn't done like that when my father was the missionary secretary'). 'Do we have to have guitars desecrating morning communion?' 'Look at how all those young people dress (or don't dress) in the evening services — it's a disgrace'.

Responses like these may be understandable, but they are little more than gut reactions. Even more troubling is the frequency with which they are spoken in a judgemental manner. They are fervently held, but all viewpoints can be fervently held by someone or some group; it is never an argument in their favour. Churches by the hundred are closing their doors as a result of attitudes like these. Emotional commitment in itself may or may not have anything to do with what it means to be a Christian. The 75-mph drivers may be anathema to some of the 70-mph drivers, but this says nothing about the validity of the 75-mph position. Unfortunately, far too many people are unable to recognize this, and they confuse holding a Christian position fervently with the truth of that position. They then find it very difficult to distinguish between a viewpoint and the people holding that viewpoint. Fervent denunciation of those holding the 'wrong' viewpoint easily opens the way to fervent denunciation of the people themselves. This was never the way of Christ, and it is not to be our way. The Lifdyl parable is far more apt than some would like it to be.

The pros and cons of being passionate

Throughout this book I've assumed something very important, and this is that all involved in these debates are thoroughly committed to the cause of Christ, and their chief end in life is to glorify God and enjoy him forever. In other words, their aims and goals are essentially the same. They are seeking to be the aroma of Christ to a world in need; their aim is to live out their professional and Christian responsibilities within a Christ-centred framework. Nevertheless, even with so much in common, it would be absurd to expect total agreement; whether it be on social priorities, political aspirations, liturgical emphases, or various points of biblical interpretation. And, like it or not, we do differ on all these points, as well as many others. What, then, becomes of Christian commitment? I'm not suggesting we abandon it — far from it, since it's of the utmost importance. I'm not arguing for a sterile intellectual faith. But we need to recognize two sides to Christian commitment. People 'on fire for the Lord' are to be admired because their hearts are in the right place, and they are determined that others should hear about Christ and all he has to offer. There may be a great deal of passion and strong feeling bound up in this, which is hardly surprising since commitment to a great cause involves all we are. This is the positive side of commitment. Unfortunately, precisely because a great deal is at stake, other people may not be allowed to question any part of their commitment. Even the slightest questioning is seen as heresy and betrayal. This is the negative side of commitment, and if this is allowed to develop too far, their commendable commitment to Christ becomes overshadowed by harsh, condemnatory attitudes that destroy those not equally committed to it in exactly the same way.

The challenge is to hold the positive and negative sides of commitment together. How can the positive side flourish without being destroyed by the negative side?

Does commitment to a good cause have to be ruined by excessive emotional commitment that cannot cope with diversity or pluralism? An inability to make this distinction indicates spiritual malaise. Once passion for a good cause and impatience with other ways of expressing it become mixed up, the focus of that passion has moved from the cause itself to the individual. The cause becomes mine and not Christ's. No matter how unintended this is, the spotlight falls on me and my esteem.

Enthusiasm for a soccer team is fine, but once that enthusiasm runs out of control, it can readily become blind passion for that team. Once the ability to look at the team's faults and failings is lost, all sense of proportion is lost. The same is true of patriotism which, when unleashed, is dangerous in the extreme; it has ceased being a virtue.

Likewise with Christians: commitment to a cause within the church must be based on integrity and truthfulness. We have responsibility to look at as many of the facts as possible, especially when disagreement is with our brothers and sisters in Christ. To think we are the only people in possession of the truth, and that all those around us in the church are in the wrong, is fraught with danger. A point is readily reached where no data will convince us we could possibly be mistaken. To end up thinking that all other Christians have been fooled is a sure sign that we ourselves have been fooled. Tragic as this is, it is even more so when we hold to our 'truth' with a passion that brooks no opposition. It would be far better if we were not passionate at all, than to let our passion lead us on a trail of broken relationships, misunderstanding, and condemnation.

From here, it is but a small step to concealing facts that do not fit our ideas. To become fervent advocates of one position, the 'correct' one, and equally fervent critics of all other positions, is to blind ourselves to the truth. Once we give up objective evaluation and openness to other perspectives, we narrow the world to that of adversaries. People like this exist and flourish because of their adversarial stance; all they do is defend the one 'correct' position, all too often at the expense of truth. But in legal systems, the role of advocate has constraints. There are ethical boundaries beyond which honest attorneys and other advocates will not go. Unfortunately, advocates for a single narrow cause all too often ignore ethical constraints; the truth suffers and falsehoods are readily fabricated.

The sadness of this situation is that young Christians brought up on a diet of excessive emphasis on one particular position, are appallingly let down if they ever begin to question the validity of that particular position. All too readily they may conclude that if they can't believe what their mentors have insisted on, how can they believe anything else within the church or in the Bible? All around us are the testimonies of those who have not survived within this environment. Once we view Christ through the narrow lens of a young earth, or a particular form of baptism, or one form of church government, we have restricted Christ to this one dimension. Of the many one-dimensional versions of Christianity, many are held with a passion that brooks no opposition. The multi-dimensional complexity and confusion of debate has been reduced to a simple 'right' answer. While applauding the intentions of those who advocate such answers, I cannot support them.

All one-dimensional versions of Christianity ignore the circle of freedom within which Christians are able to move. Whenever confronted by peripheral issues, we have to acknowledge this biblical circle of freedom within which Christians may operate with faithfulness and integrity. To deny the existence of such a circle of freedom, and to restrict Christians to a fixed point (*my* 'correct' interpretation of Scripture), is to limit the work of Christ.

Think of someone who believes that church members are the only ones in a position to appoint the minister.

However, the local landowner appoints the minister in this particular parish. For our friend this is akin to a denial of the headship of Christ over his church. She is aghast. A central issue in her Christianity is under threat. She longs to be faithful to Christ; she wants to see Christ as the church's head. All is at stake. She is passionate about this appalling development and, with all the vigour she can muster, she gives everything she has to this cause, regardless of the consequences. Her heart is in the right place, but her commitment to the cause overrides all else. If she is to prevent disaster ensuing, she will have to stand back and examine the merits of the situation within the broader framework of her and other people's commitment to Christ. The arrangement for appointing ministers in this situation may be far from ideal (or biblical?), but is this really of ultimate importance? The faithfulness of the minister, no matter how appointed, the unity of Christ's body, and the witness of the community come first. It is a different matter if the minister strays far from biblical truth; but that is another story.

There's no doubting our friend's spiritual commitment; there's no doubting her strength of feeling. But she is wrong. Her devotion to the lordship of Christ may readily become a self-righteous opinionated stance. Look at other Christians — they are faithful without this position. It is misleading to argue that Christ is less Lord over all these other people's lives. Be pragmatic. Look around; open your eyes. Be honest. Don't fudge the data. And don't be so inward-looking and narrow. Be open to the Spirit of Christ in other Christians, as well as in yourself.

This issue is a peripheral one. To make it central is to fall into all those traps I've been discussing in this book. Ignorance and bigotry have never converted a peripheral issue into a central one; and strength of feeling, deep emotional commitment, and passion can all cloud the picture.

Should there be boundaries?

We may conclude that our biblical interpretation on
some important matter is essentially correct and that it is
crucial to our Christian position. And so we have to
separate from those with a different interpretation of the
issue in question. Alternatively, we may decide that,
even though we consider our position as essentially
correct and others as incorrect, the unity of the body of
Christ is more important. And so we are obliged to
maintain fellowship and keep open lines of communication with those whom we consider wrong on this one
issue.

This choice is a theological one and it is fundamental,
determining how we carry on debate with our opponents in Christ. My own position is that we are con-
strained by Christ to maintain the unity we have in him,
whatever the pressures and limitations placed upon us
by this constraint. The differences between groups are
those of normal vitality rather than tragic dissension. We
should praise the Lord that, different as we are, we can
look each other in the face and recognize a redeemed
image of God. Such acceptance may be far from easy,
and does not come readily to many of us, especially
when we long to be faithful to our Lord.

The matters I've raised throughout this book have
consequences for churches. Throughout, I have been
pointing in the direction of openness, an openness that
should also characterize our churches. But this is where
difficulties abound. Churches, as much as individuals,
love labels. They are known by labels: charismatic, non-
charismatic, Reformed, Baptist, Anglican. Churches are
recognized as having a healing ministry, they see themselves as being worshipping communities, they are faith
centres. They are Pentecostal, or holiness churches, they
are pre-tribulation or postmillenial, they are fundament-
alist, they believe in an inerrant Bible. All labels are
limiting, no matter how well-intentioned. What is important are the attitudes of churches, and how firmly or

otherwise they cling to the labels. The more firmly they do, the less openness they display on secondary matters.

So often there are also hidden barriers. People are not welcome because they hang loose when it comes to certain tenets of belief of that particular church — they hold the 'wrong' view on baptism, they believe in an old earth when the pastor preaches that a young earth viewpoint is the only one true to the gospel, they are not strict pro-lifers in a church politically and spiritually aligned to the pro-life movement, they are open to women in leadership positions when the stance of the church is in favour of male-only leadership. Problem areas are sometimes even more subtle: people who ask questions in a church with authoritarian leaders, people with doubts and unresolved questions in a church where doubt is frowned upon, single mothers in a family-oriented church, the unemployed in a church with largely professional members, poorly educated in a church with a predominance of highly educated parishioners.

Then there are personality clashes. While I have not dealt with these, they can be dressed in other garb. What are essentially personality differences can be made to look 'spiritual', as though the disagreement is over important matters, not simply likes and dislikes. People who don't quite fit in can be accused of unworthy motives; they may have 'unspecified problems'. There are means of casting them to one side, so that their criticisms or suggestions don't have to be taken seriously. They are sidelined and dismissed.

In all these instances, boundaries are being erected — allowing some people in, and keeping others out. None of these boundaries has anything to do with the heart of the gospel.

Only one conclusion can be drawn from all I have written, and this is that churches should be far more open than they frequently are. Openness on secondary issues is no reason why Christ should not be just as central as in churches with rigid boundaries. Openness occurs where a diversity of beliefs and expression is allowed on secondary matters; even encouraged. It is seen in a lack of emphasis on those features that divide us. Biblical teaching should be crucial; the Bible, faithfully and rigorously expounded, applied diligently and vigorously, with widespread discussion of the implications of biblical teaching for lifestyle and moral values. And yet, there is an openness to each other.

Churches that are open in this manner are frequently characterized by their ability to attract Christians from a wide variety of church and denominational backgrounds. They tend to attract non-Christians, or those with little grasp of the faith. People are welcomed, even when sometimes they don't fit in. There is a warm and accepting environment. This doesn't mean there are no boundaries. There are, and church discipline may be imposed. But the boundaries are made as unobtrusive as possible. The driving force behind such churches is that nothing should displace the centrality of Christ as Lord and Saviour, and as Creator and Redeemer.

There are dangers in such openness. Control is less easy than when rigid, clear-cut, neat boundaries are erected. There will be fuzzy edges. But the dangers are minimized as long as Christ is central, and as long as the Bible is taken seriously as the one and only measure of Christian truth. An openness to each other is possible because of an openness to God and to the Holy Spirit. Openness, such as I have been describing, is the openness of faith and hope.

Which of us hasn't a few minor heresies?

'What a question! Of course, I haven't any heresies! I'm sound; I'm biblical'. How many of us will respond to my intemperate question in this way? But think again. Do we really consider that everything we believe is assured? Is everything true to the Bible?

Put like this, we may have a few shocks. Much as we take the teaching of the Bible seriously, we must know that there are rough edges — points about which we are unsure, points where we have changed our mind, points where we are bemused. Of course, we all have some minor heresies — we may not be sure what they are, but they are there.

Those who are unwilling to admit that they have any heresies (however small) have become cult-like in their faith. They have so circumscribed it, that it has become rigid and inflexible: what a tragic state of affairs. What room is there for learning, for growing in the faith, for extending the boundaries of our understanding? Growth is one of the most joyous and privileged aspects of the Christian faith. We are to learn from others — including those not quite like us. We are to appreciate those who are different from us. We are to rejoice in those with different heresies from ourselves. We are to welcome those who have been strangers up to now.

People incapable of further growth have developed spiritual senility. They have fossilized. As we grow we welcome each other, and we learn from each other. If I have some heresies, I need to learn from you who don't have the same ones. I don't know everything. Above all, I long to know Christ better.

Making ourselves vulnerable

If we act in the ways I've been proposing both in this chapter and throughout the book, there will be a repercussion. We make ourselves vulnerable — to criticism, alternative and challenging ideas, and the questioning of our motives and goals. As soon as we treat others as being on the same level as ourselves, we invite their contributions. We ask them to provide ideas and thoughts, and perhaps the ones they come up with will be at variance with our own. Rather than protecting ourselves from the onslaught of others, we expose ourselves as we invite comments and contributions. We make ourselves vulnerable.

This is implicit in all dialogue, and it's basic to Christian attitudes. Christ could have shielded himself from the questioning and probing of the sceptics of his day, and yet he invited their comments and questions. He debated with the Pharisees and Sadduces; he turned their trick questions to his own advantage, and he elicited supremely important teaching from scurrilously ambivalent queries. He healed in defiance of the strictures of the Pharisees since he considered that the person in need of healing was more important than the regulations emanating from the Pharisees. As he spoke to people, including those at the periphery of respectable society, and as he allowed some of these to express their response to him, his values and priorities became clear.

By entering into debate in this way, Jesus made himself vulnerable, since he exposed his teaching and his message about who he was to the scrutiny of those who were the most ardent exponents of an alternative tradition. What is significant is that it was in doing this that Jesus conveyed much of his important teaching. What emerged out of the tumult of dialogue was a clear picture of who Jesus was, what he was like, and the way to the kingdom of God. For Jesus there was no hiding behind a pulpit or lectern, nor behind prestigious titles or degrees. Rather, he entered into meaningful relationships with ordinary people. Having humbled himself and become an ordinary human being (Phil. 2:5–11), he ensured that his dealings were predominantly with ordinary people. He continued to be vulnerable throughout the whole of his earthly existence.

This principle of vulnerability sums up much of my message in this book. Every specific recommendation I've put forward leads to vulnerability — whether this be through dialogue, openness, mutual interdependence, accountability, servanthood, refusing to question the motives of our opponents, or praying for those who criticize us. It is the *sine qua non* of the Christian life.

Take an illustration.

> Imagine a church in which the pastor reckons that the present church building should be demolished and replaced by a larger one, better suited to the size and needs of the present growing congregation. He could tell the leaders and congregation that this is what will be done, and that schemes for raising the necessary finances should be implemented immediately. He ignores any dissent within the congregation, and allows no discussion of the matter. On the other hand, he could let the congregation know about his plans and hopes, encourage them to discuss it openly, to pray about it, and to come up with their own questions, concerns, and expectations. In doing this, he is seeking their support, response, and further initiatives. His fervent hope is that, together, they will find the mind of the Lord and discover his way forward — even if it be a decision to refrain from going ahead with the building plans.

The second approach lays the pastor open to criticism. He is making himself vulnerable. He may be hurt by lack of support and rejection of his ideas. The first approach avoids this. And yet, it is only the second approach that takes the concerns of others seriously, that is willing to accept other legitimate viewpoints, and that may benefit from the contribution of the concerned parties. Any controversy that surfaces should be put to positive use, to be of value to all involved.

Vulnerability is the way to strength and wisdom. It may not be the easy way, but it is far more akin to the example of Jesus than the first approach is. To make oneself vulnerable is the way of the cross.

In praise of dissent

Throughout this book, I have argued that dissent can be a positive virtue. Dissent lies at the heart of controversy, and so by implication I recognize that controversy itself may be put to beneficial uses. It can be constructive rather than destructive. But is this really possible, or am I advocating a fool's dream? At best, dissent encourages thinking and a serious approach to Bible study. It encourages Christians to take up their responsibilities and to work out ways in which the Bible can help them come to grips with the pressures and challenges of all sorts of everyday issues. Rather than sit back and be told what the 'correct' perspective is, it encourages a serious approach to viable alternatives and drives them to rely on the Holy Spirit for wisdom. This does not make them totally independent, but it does stress their responsibility before God for being faithful stewards of what he has given them.

Dissent encourages openness, dialogue, and discussion, and discourages authoritarian structures within an organization. Openness may be difficult to handle at times, and yet it is the way to new ideas and proposals. The resurgence of evangelicalism in recent years had its origins in a dissenting movement. Without dissent there is no new life.

Even within a group where all are working from the same basic principles and are committed to the same fundamentals, dissent can be productive. It allows the flowering of ideas and practices, and the exploration of new ways. Without it, the interpretation of the leader(s) is the only possible interpretation, and this may be limiting. After all, why assume that one person (or one homogeneous group) knows the mind of God perfectly? We can learn from dissent, since it may point to deficiencies in our present stance. We need to be forced to re-examine ourselves, our motives, our preconceptions, and our goals. Dissent can help us do these things. We may not change any of them, but re-examination can be very healthy.

Above all, we need to beware of indulging in any form of intellectual or spiritual suppression, since this leads to dishonesty and, at its worst, to ruthless oppression. It can happen in any situation, including a Christian one, and is a tendency we have to check repeatedly. We need to learn that *authoritarianism and suppression are worse than dissent*. When we compare the Pharisees on the one hand to Jesus on the other, we emerge with a clear picture of the contrast. Authoritarianism and suppression led to the crucifixion of Jesus, whereas the dissent that Jesus allowed in those around him led to a total transformation of their lives.

The trouble is that, for so long, we've been used to monolithic denominations and sect-like expressions of Christianity which don't encourage dissent within them. It's true that there is considerable dissent in some instances, but even these are frequently seen as being aberrations that should not occur. We have also found it difficult to distinguish dissent over central beliefs and peripheral matters, and so attitudes towards the latter have had much in common with attitudes towards the former. I am no advocate of a plethora of denominations and church groupings, especially when they mirror the personality, likes and dislikes of one person, their human founder. However, some of these developments have probably been the result of our difficulty in coping creatively and positively with dissent.

This book started out as a response to the problems created by controversy. At the time I saw controversy in essentially negative terms. And yet, as I've coped with it and pondered its character, I've come to see the positive elements of dissent. We all have much to learn about how best to come to terms with differences in opinions and attitudes, but for Christians the only legitimate approach is provided by a Christ-centred perspective. Once this is the controlling influence for all our thinking and attitudes, we are well on the way to coping with controversy, and putting it to good use.

The challenge of Lifdyl

The 70-mph Christians have two options. They could exclude the 75-mph Christians from their fellowship

because of what they regard as the fundamental differences between them, or they learn to accept the 75-mph
Christians as fellow-workers even though they have
disagreements on this matter (exceedingly important as
it may be in their eyes). The 75-mph Christians need to
look very closely at their stance in view of the profound
concern shown by their 70-mph fellow-believers. After
all, they may be wrong; perhaps they have been too
liberal in their interpretation of this matter. Together,
though, they are to assess the bases of their respective
positions against those of other Lifdylians, travelling
well in excess of 100 mph, and totally ignoring the
strictures of both the 70- and 75-mph Christian groups.
The challenge for both Christian groups is to seek the
Lord, and by their integrity, honesty, uprightness and
creative holiness to demonstrate to the remaining Lifdylians that their way and their ethical imperatives are
compelling. This is only possible if they build on the
unity they have in Christ, rejoicing in their diversity, and
ensuring that servanthood underpins every aspect of
their lives as Christ's people.

But why not take another approach? Why not gladly
accept that those who drive at different speeds from us
have something to say to us? Why not welcome this
difference and make the most of it? Don't reject it and
treat it as a threat. It's good to be slightly different
(within the 70–75 mph range); we can learn from others,
and they may well bring a freshness and verve to us. We
have something to learn from each other. Enjoy each
other and what we represent. Enjoy our differences.

To many this will be heresy. Please remember that I'm
still discussing differences over secondary matters, just
as I have been throughout this book. What I'm now
advocating is that we don't just tolerate those who differ
from us on minor matters, but that we learn to enjoy
what they are and have to offer. This requires education,
and for most of us a serious effort to get outside our
narrow cloisters, and experience what other Christians
are like.

We don't agree on all points, and we never will. But as they love the same Lord we love, we have something to learn from them. We may still feel more comfortable with those who are like us — have our attitudes, our theological niceties, our outlook on life, our do's and don'ts. That's fine. But why can't we rub shoulders with those who are a little unlike us, who have slightly different views on the second coming, baptism, the role of the organ in church services, the number of pastors in the church, the necessity or otherwise for men to wear ties or jeans in church services, the age of the earth, or women in church leadership?

Perhaps we still don't want to tackle matters like this. Perhaps we still long for homogeneity. Forget about controversy. Pretend it doesn't exist. Pull up the ramparts; forget about those Christians who are awkward and who don't agree with us. I assume that if you have read this far, you will be beyond this response, or have totally given up on my approach.

A friend of mine wrote to me after reading the first edition of this book: 'Who wants to proceed cautiously (or even biblically) when one's dander is up for any reason (good or bad)? And when one's dander is not up, why take a thoughtful position on how to handle controversy?' That puts it in a nutshell. But that cannot be the end. However much sin affects the mind, however much we may be tempted to ignore this whole issue, it's central to the nature and functioning of Christ's church. And that means we cannot ignore it, and we cannot ignore those other Christians who insist on being rebellious Lifdylians.

Questions for group discussion

1. Talk about the Lifdyl illustration. Do you think it makes a valid point? Or does it irritate you? Why do you think you respond as you do?

2. How do you cope with someone in your church who makes it obvious that they are very enthusiastic about what they believe, especially when you disagree with their stance?

3. The term 'circle of freedom' is mentioned in the section on 'The pros and cons of being passionate'. Discuss whether you think this is a useful idea.

4. To what extent should we use labels for ourselves and others? Are labels a help or a hindrance?

5. How 'open' or 'closed' should churches be? Advocate one or other of these positions, and think of biblical reasons for them.

6. Discuss the value of dissent within Christian circles.

Books for Further Reading

Controversy

Robert Ames, *One in the Truth?* Eastbourne: Kingsway, 1988

David Coffey, *Build that Bridge*, Eastbourne: Kingsway, 1986

Horace L Fenton, *When Christians Clash*, Downers Grove: Inter-Varsity Press, 1987

Brian Hatherway, *Living Below with the Saints we Know*, Auckland: N-Joy Publishing, 1996

Robert Moeller, *Love in Action*, Sisters, Oregon: Multnomah Books, 1994

Richard T Mouw, *Uncommon Decency*, Downers Grove: Inter-Varsity Press, 1992

James and Nina Rye, *The Survivor's Guide to Church Life*, Leicester: Inter-Varsity Press, 1992

Gerald L. Sittser, *Loving Across our Differences*, Downers Grove, Illinois: Inter-Varsity Press, 1994

John White and Ken Blue, *Healing the Wounded*, Leicester: Inter-Varsity Press, 1985

Evangelicalism

Oliver R Barclay, *Whatever Happened to the Jesus Lane Lot?* Leicester: Inter-Varsity Press, 1977

James I Packer, *'Fundamentalism' and the Word of God*, Leicester: Inter-Varsity Press, 1958

Iain Murray, *D Martyn Lloyd-Jones*, vol. 1, 2, Edinburgh: Banner of Truth, 1982, 1990

Donald G Bloesch, *The Evangelical Renaissance*, Grand Rapids: Eerdmans, 1973

Carl F H Henry, *The Uneasy Conscience of Modern Fundamentalism*, Grand Rapids: Eerdmans, 1947

Carl F H Henry, *Evangelicals in Search of Identity*, Waco: Word Books, 1976

Richard Quebedeaux, *The Worldly Evangelicals*, New York: Harper and Row, 1978

Bernard L Ramm, *The Evangelical Heritage*, Waco: Word Books, 1973

Illustrations of evangelical thinking

Fred Catherwood, *At the Cutting Edge*, London: Hodder and Stoughton, 1995

Timothy Dudley-Smith (ed.), *Authentic Christianity*, Downers Grove, Illinois: Inter-Varsity Press, 1995

Martyn Eden and David F Wells (eds), *The Gospel in the Modern World*, Leicester/Downers Grove: Inter-Varsity Press, 1991

Carl F H Henry, *Confessions of a Theologian*, Waco: Word Books, 1986

Donald M MacKay (edited by Melvin Tinker), *The Open Mind and Other Essays*, Leicester: Inter-Varsity Press, 1988

George M Marsden, *Reforming Fundamentalism*, Grand Rapids: Eerdmans, 1987

John Stott, *Issues Facing Christians Today*, Basingstoke: Marshalls, 1984

Controversy, Censorship and Intellectual Suppresion

S D Gaede, *When Tolerance is no Virtue*, Downers Grove, Illinois: Inter-Varsity Press, 1993

Richard McCormick, *How Brave a New World?* London: SCM Press, 1981

Donald M MacKay, 'The health of the evangelical body', *Journal of the American Scientific Affiliation* 38: pp 258–65 (1986)

B Martin, C M A Baker, C Manwell and C Pugh (eds), *Intellectual Suppression*, Sydney: Angus and Robertson, 1986

John Milton, *Areopagitica* in *Complete Poems and Major Prose* (ed M Y Hughes), New York: Odyssey Press, 1957

James Sire, 'Brave new publishers: Should they be censored?' in 'Evangelicalism: Surviving its Success' (ed David A Fraser) *The Evangelical Round Table*, vol. 2, Eastern College and Eastern Baptist Theological Seminary, St Davids, Pennsylvania, 1987, pp 128–47

Cal Thomas, *Book Burning*, Westchester, Illinois: Crossway, 1983

Index of Scripture References

Psalms
141:5   96

Proverbs
9:7–9   96

Matthew
5:13–16   99, 107
5:17–48   54
6   51
7   52, 53
7:1–6   47
7:15–20   53
12:1–14   105
12:33–37   54
13:24–30   55
15:1–9   54, 86, 105
16:23   96
17:17   96
18:1–5, 10–14   62
18:15–17   56

18:15–17, 19,
   20   64
18:21–35   69
22:15–22   55
22:23–33   55
23   51
23:1–12,
   23–28, 33   50
26:6–13   56
26:20–25   96
26:45, 46   96

Mark
4:40   96
7:17–19   96
8:14–21   96
14:1–10   96
14:37–41   96

Luke
9:46–48   96

9:51–56	96
10:25–37	100
11:37–44	105
14:7–14	78
22:48	96

John
6:70, 71	96
7:19–24	87
8:1–11	105
13:1–11	84
13:10, 11	96
13:10–21	96
13:26–30	96
17:20–23	74

Acts
| 15 | 67 |
| 15:36–41 | 68 |

Romans
12:3, 4	78
12:4–8	74
14:1–10, 13–22	58
15:1, 2	58

1 Corinthians
3:1–3	139
3:1–9	89
5:12, 13	94
12:1–31	75
12:12–31	74, 117
14:1–39	75

2 Corinthians
| 5:15 | 84 |

Galatians
| 3:1–4:11 | 119 |
| 4:21–5:1 | 119 |

5:13–18	119
5:19	88
5:20	87
5:20, 21	88
5:22–25	88
6:1, 2	96
6:12	87

Ephesians
4:1–6	74
4:7–16	74
4:11–13	75
4:25, 32	85
4:29	85
4:29–5:2	100

Philippians
1:12–18	79
1:27–30	80
2:1, 2	80
2:3, 4	78
2:3–11	82
2:5–11	160
4:2, 3	66

Colossians
2:16	86
2:20–33	92
2:21–23	86

1 Thessalonians
| 5:13, 14 | 100 |

1 Timothy
1:4	92
3:1–13	109
5:19–21	100
6:4–5	92
6:20	100

2 Timothy
2:24   94
2:23, 24   92

Titus
3:9   92, 94

James
3:9–4:3   85
4:11, 12   94

1 Peter
3:8   100

1 John
4:1–4   97
4:7–12   100

3 John
9, 10   85